Bedtime BIBLE Stories

Autumn House

Bedtime Bible Stories

First published by
Scandinavia Publishing House 2017
Drejervej 15, 3., DK-2400 Copenhagen NV, Denmark
info@sph.as | www.sph.as

Text and illustrations copyright © Scandinavia Publishing House

Illustrations by Fabiano Fiorin

Text by Vanessa Carroll

Edited by Cecilie Fodor & Sherry Brown

Cover design by Svetlana Uscumlic

Book layout by Gao Hanyu

This edition published, with permission, by Autumn House Publications (Europe) Ltd, in 2018

Copyright © 2018

Printed in China

ISBN 978-1-78665-970-5

All rights reserved. No part of this book may be reproduced or utilised in any form or by any means, electronic or mechanical, including photocopying, recording, or by any information storage and retrieval system, without permission in writing from the publisher.

Contents

The Boy Whose Dreams Came True 5

The Prince Whom God Chose to Be His Servant 19

The Shepherd Who Feared Nothing 33

The Foreign Girl Who Became a Brave Queen 47

The Man Whose God Was Stronger than the Lions 61

The Sulking Prophet Who Learned About God's Forgiveness 75

The Son Who Thought He Knew Better 89

The Man Who Went Through the Roof 103

The Greedy Man Who Started to Share 115

The Dead Girl Who Came Back to Life 127

The Boy Whose Dreams Came True

Genesis 37 & 39–45

Joseph was the second-youngest in his family. His father, Jacob, treated him differently than his older brothers by giving him special attention and gifts.

The brothers were very jealous of him because they knew Joseph was their father's favourite.

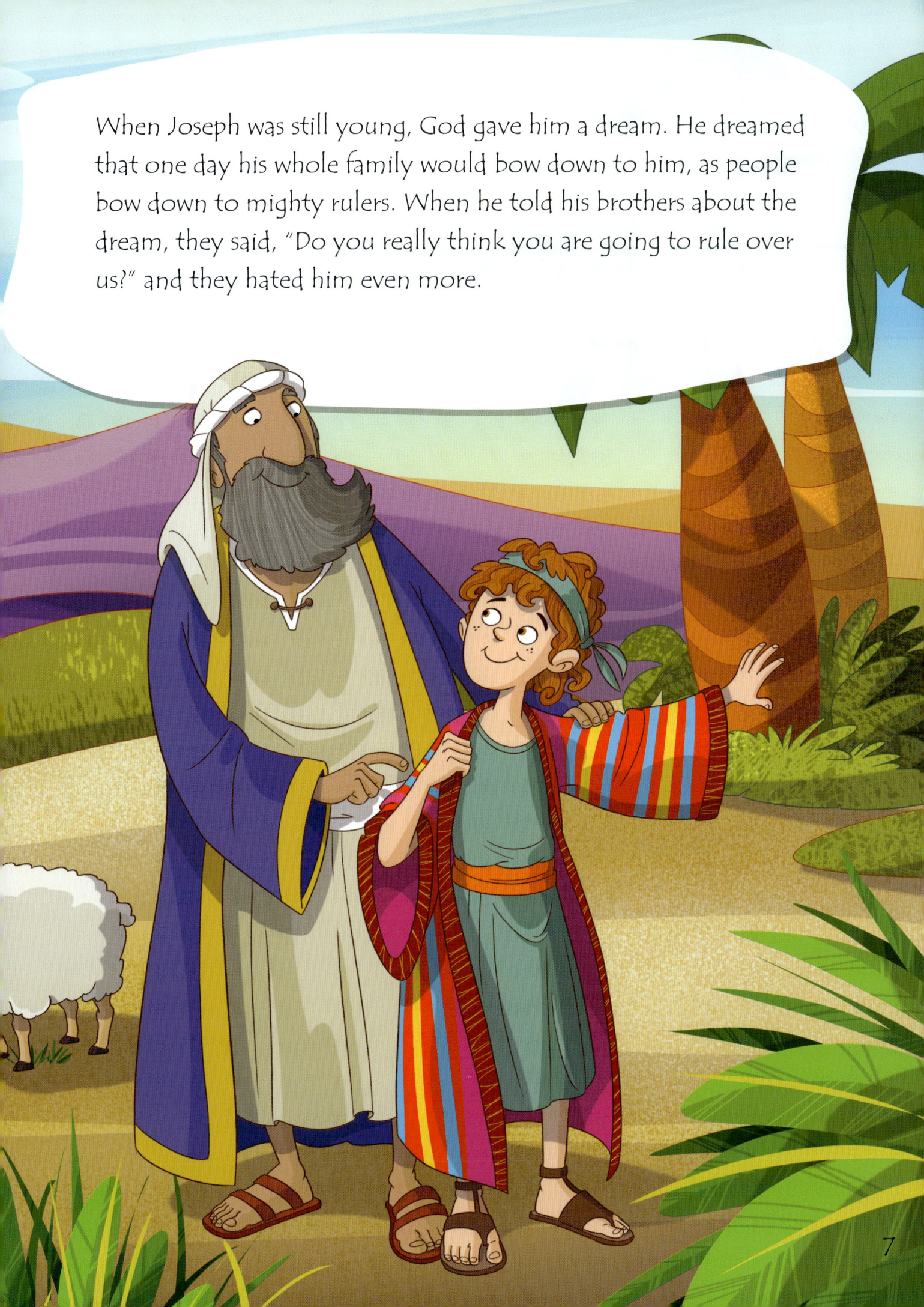

When Joseph was still young, God gave him a dream. He dreamed that one day his whole family would bow down to him, as people bow down to mighty rulers. When he told his brothers about the dream, they said, "Do you really think you are going to rule over us?" and they hated him even more.

One day, Joseph was sent to check on his brothers as they were working. When they saw him coming, they said, "Let's get rid of the boy dreamer once and for all!" They threw him into a dried-up well and sat down to eat. Then they saw a bunch of traders coming and decided to sell Joseph as a slave.

When Joseph got to Egypt, he was bought by a powerful man named Potiphar. God was with Joseph, and Potiphar noticed that Joseph was successful in everything he did. Because Joseph always did his best and worked hard, Potiphar put Joseph in charge of everything he owned.

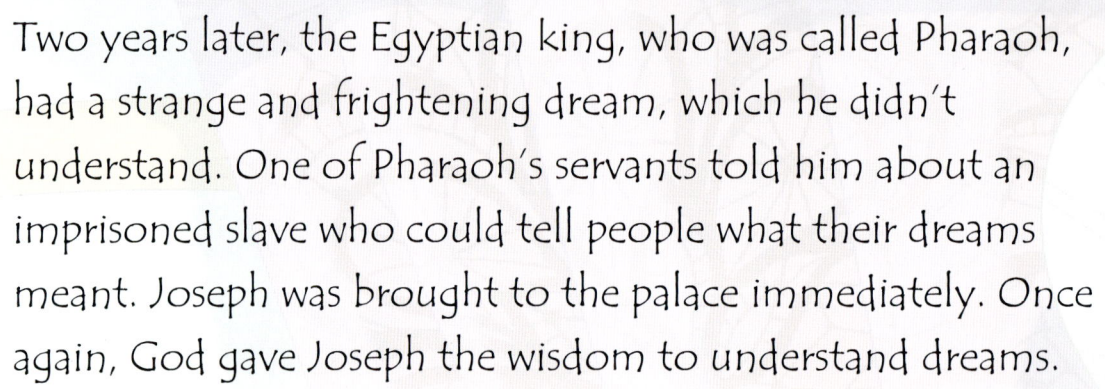

Two years later, the Egyptian king, who was called Pharaoh, had a strange and frightening dream, which he didn't understand. One of Pharaoh's servants told him about an imprisoned slave who could tell people what their dreams meant. Joseph was brought to the palace immediately. Once again, God gave Joseph the wisdom to understand dreams.

"There were seven fat cows and seven full heads of grain in your dream," said Joseph, "so there will be seven years with plenty of food in Egypt. Then came seven skinny cows and seven thin heads of grain, so there will be seven years of famine after that." Joseph advised Pharaoh to store up some food from the good years, to eat it when the bad years would come.

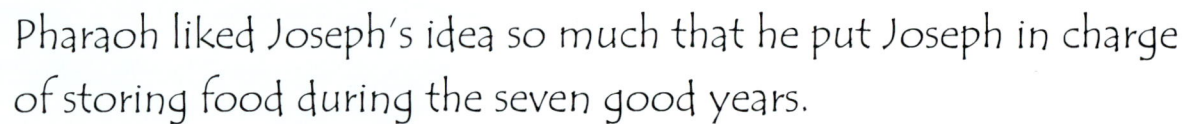

Pharaoh liked Joseph's idea so much that he put Joseph in charge of storing food during the seven good years.

After a while, when the famine had begun, Joseph's ten older brothers came to buy food, too. They didn't recognise Joseph and they bowed down to him, just like Joseph had seen them do in his dream when he was a boy.

Joseph was surprised to see them and pretended he didn't know who they were. To find out if they were still as mean as before or if they were sorry for what they had done to him, he said, "If you are good people, and not spies, bring your youngest brother here, too."

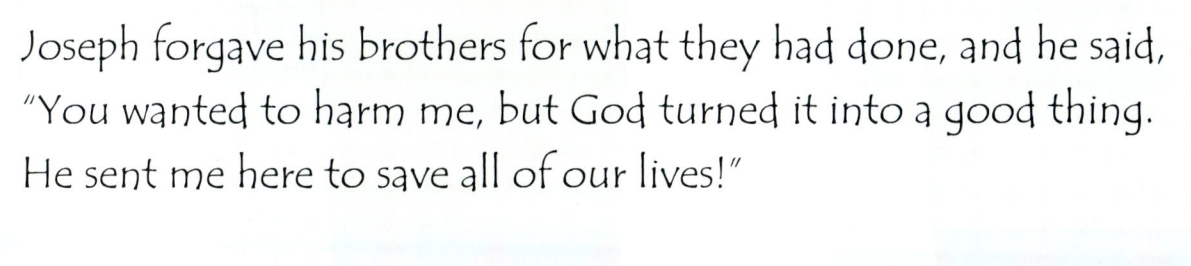

Joseph forgave his brothers for what they had done, and he said, "You wanted to harm me, but God turned it into a good thing. He sent me here to save all of our lives!"

The Prince Whom God Chose to Be His Servant

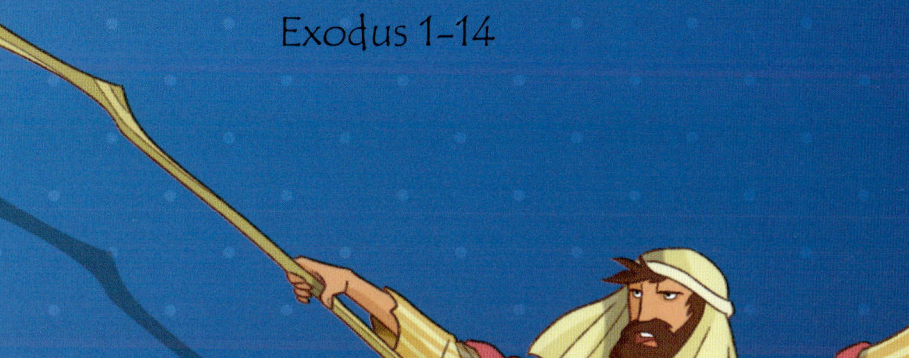

Exodus 1–14

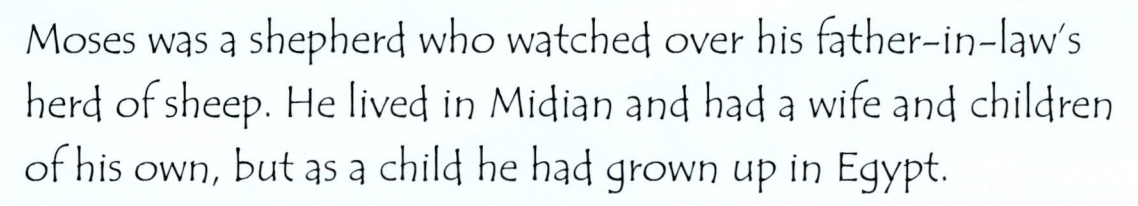

Moses was a shepherd who watched over his father-in-law's herd of sheep. He lived in Midian and had a wife and children of his own, but as a child he had grown up in Egypt.

Even though he was born a Hebrew, he had been raised by a daughter of the Egyptian King, Pharaoh. She had saved him when her father had commanded that all Hebrew baby boys were to be killed.

Now here he was, the grandson of the Pharaoh, a shepherd far away in Midian.

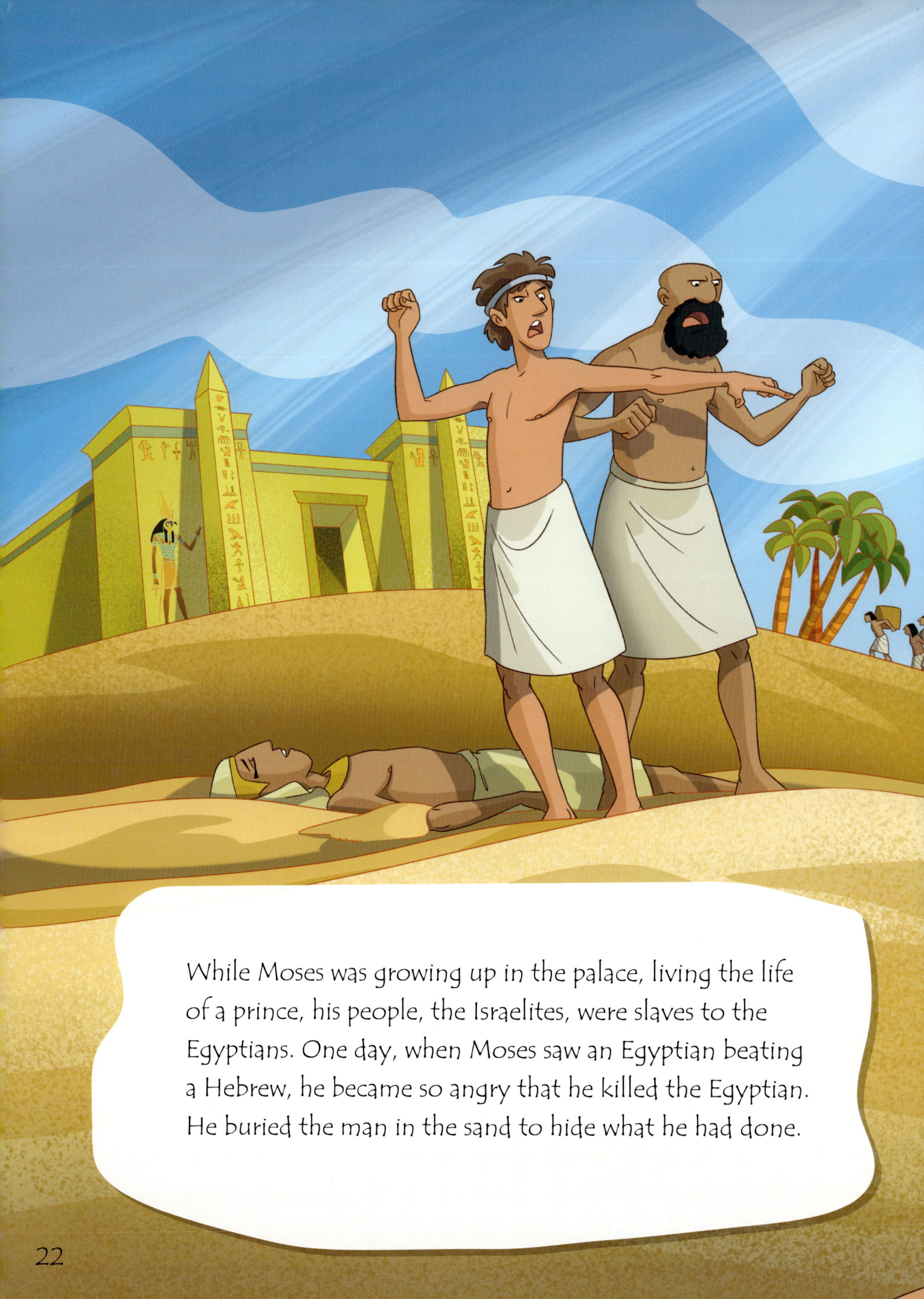

While Moses was growing up in the palace, living the life of a prince, his people, the Israelites, were slaves to the Egyptians. One day, when Moses saw an Egyptian beating a Hebrew, he became so angry that he killed the Egyptian. He buried the man in the sand to hide what he had done.

When Pharaoh heard about it, he tried to kill Moses, but Moses got away and fled to Midian. It was here that he started working as a shepherd and met Zipporah, who became his wife.

One day, Moses saw a bush on fire and went to look. From inside the bush a voice called, "Moses! Moses! I am the God of Abraham, Isaac, and Jacob." Moses hid his face, afraid to look at God.

"Go to Pharaoh in Egypt, and tell him to let My people go," God said.

"I'm not good at speaking," Moses said. "Can you find someone else?"

"Your brother, Aaron, can speak for you," God replied. "He is on his way now to meet you."

Aaron and Moses then went to Pharaoh to make him release all his slaves.

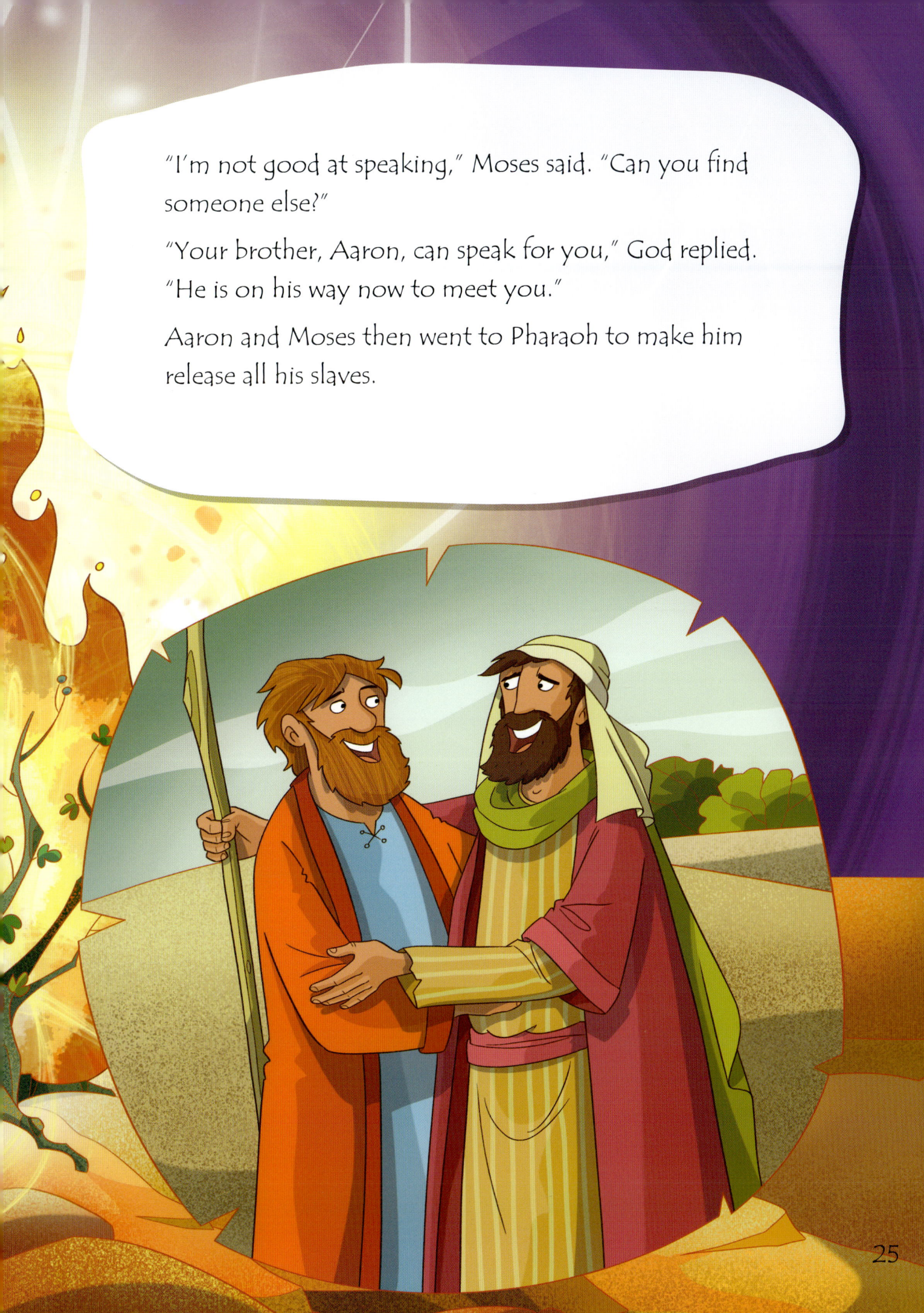

Moses and Aaron warned Pharaoh that if he didn't let the Hebrew slaves go, God would turn all water in Egypt into blood. But Pharaoh said, "No!" God sent more plagues: frogs, bugs, flies, sick animals, sores, hail, locusts, and darkness. Each time, Pharaoh still refused.

Finally, God sent a plague that killed all firstborn sons of every Egyptian family. Pharaoh's son died, too. Pharaoh then realised that God was too powerful for him. "Leave!" he shouted, "take everything and go!"

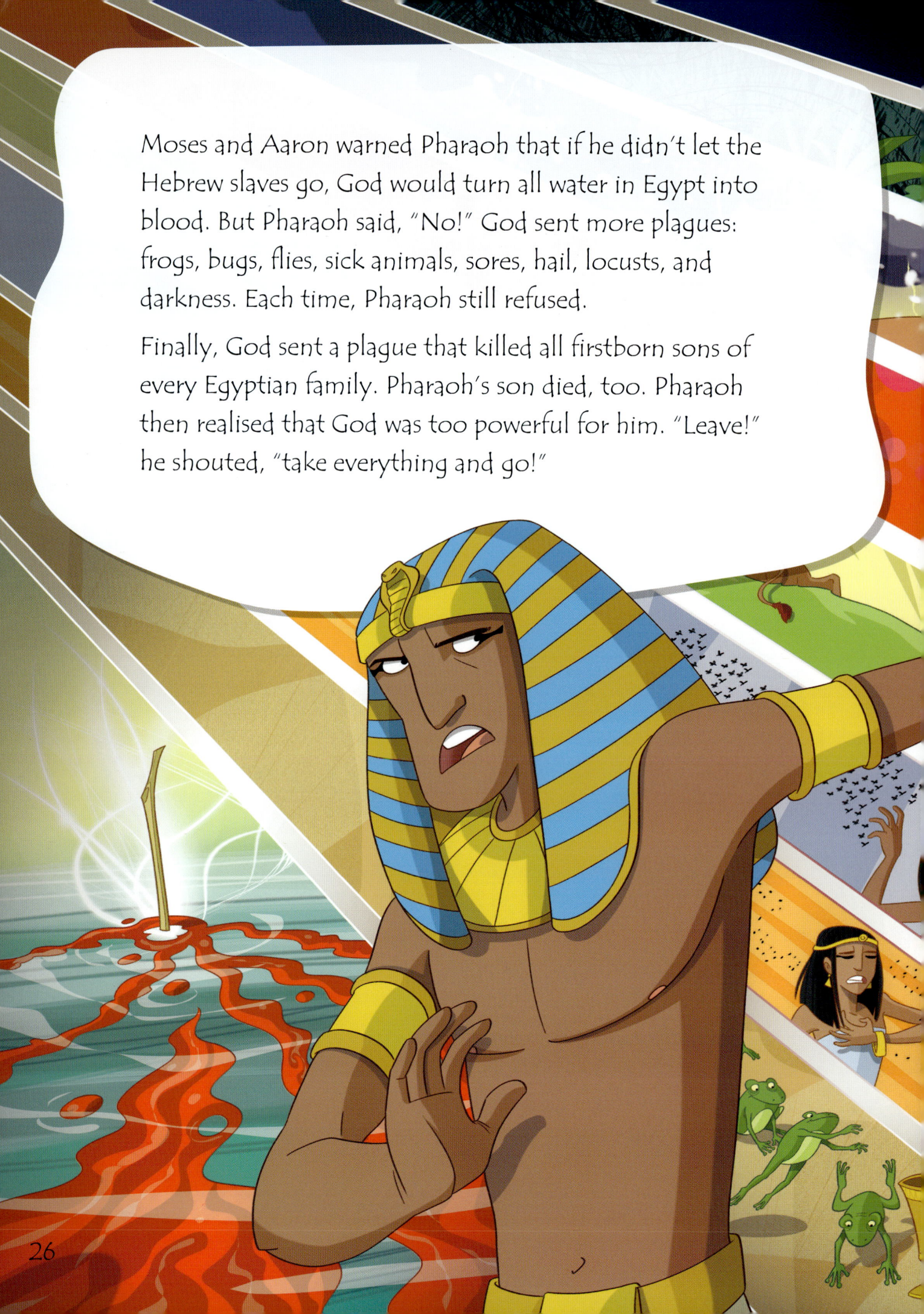

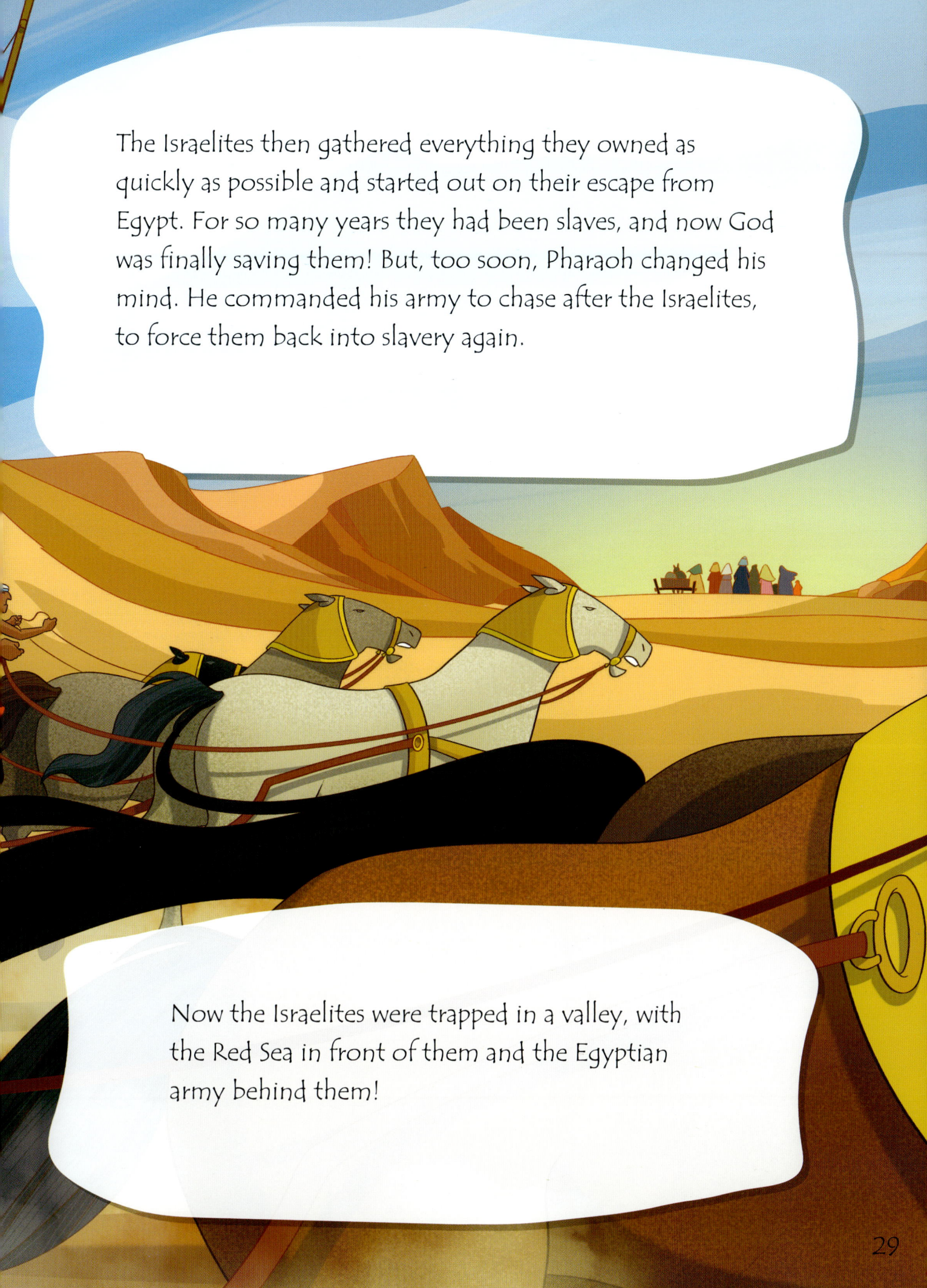

The Israelites then gathered everything they owned as quickly as possible and started out on their escape from Egypt. For so many years they had been slaves, and now God was finally saving them! But, too soon, Pharaoh changed his mind. He commanded his army to chase after the Israelites, to force them back into slavery again.

Now the Israelites were trapped in a valley, with the Red Sea in front of them and the Egyptian army behind them!

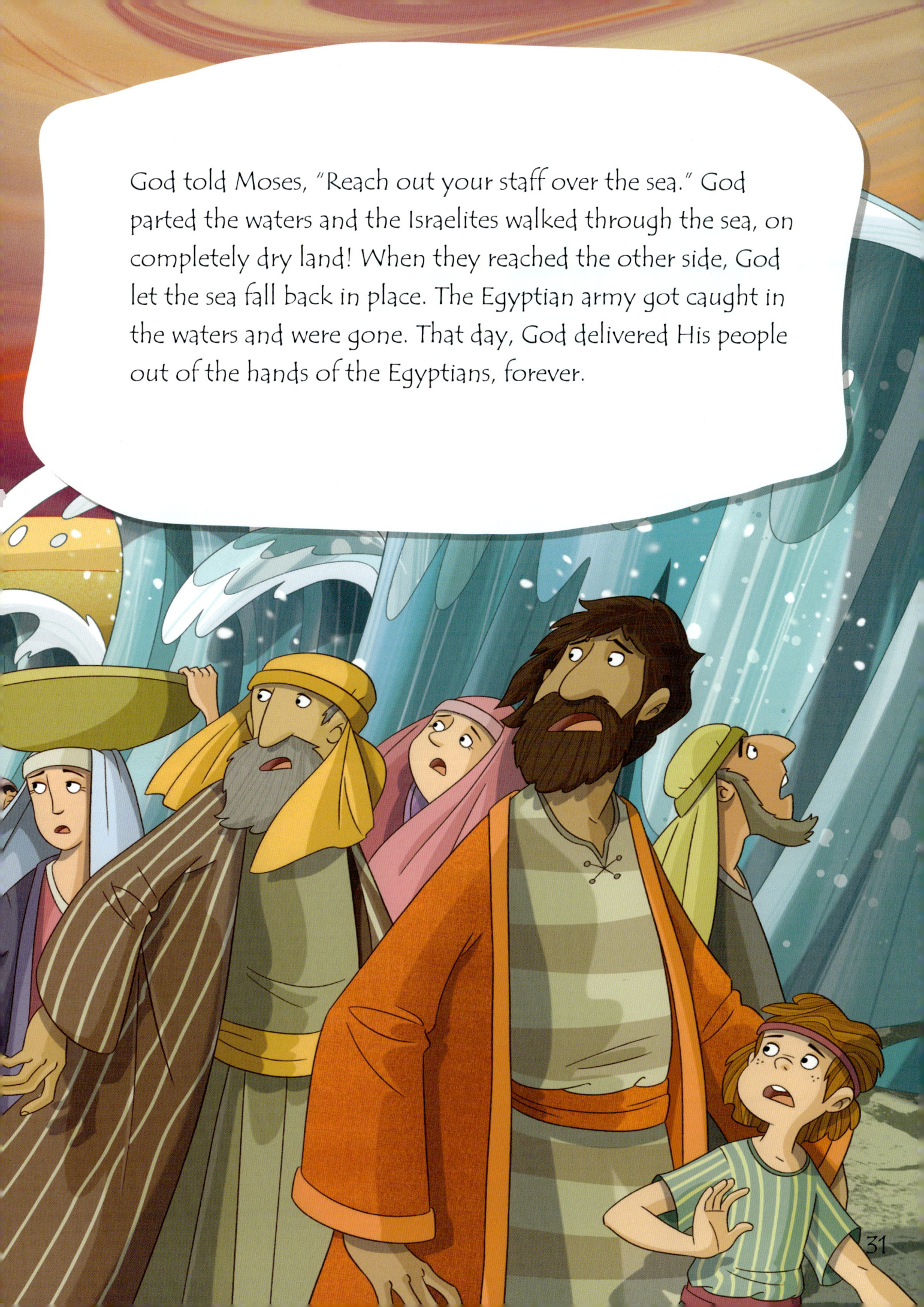

The Shepherd Who Feared Nothing

1 Samuel 16–17

David was the youngest son in his family. Three of his seven older brothers were in the Israelite army, fighting with King Saul against the Philistines. One day, David's father gathered some food for his older sons and asked David to bring it to them.

As David got to the army and found his brothers, a giant Philistine, named Goliath, came out to taunt them. He did this every day, making the Israelite army lose all courage. Everyone shrank back as Goliath came forward, wearing heavy armour and looking impossible to defeat.

"Give me a man to fight!" bellowed Goliath to the Israelites. "If your man wins, we will become your slaves. But if I win, you will become our slaves and serve us!"

No one was brave enough to fight Goliath, even though King Saul had offered a reward for killing the giant. The winner would even get to marry King Saul's daughter!

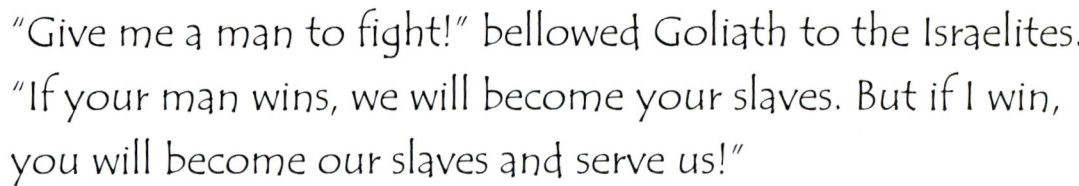

37

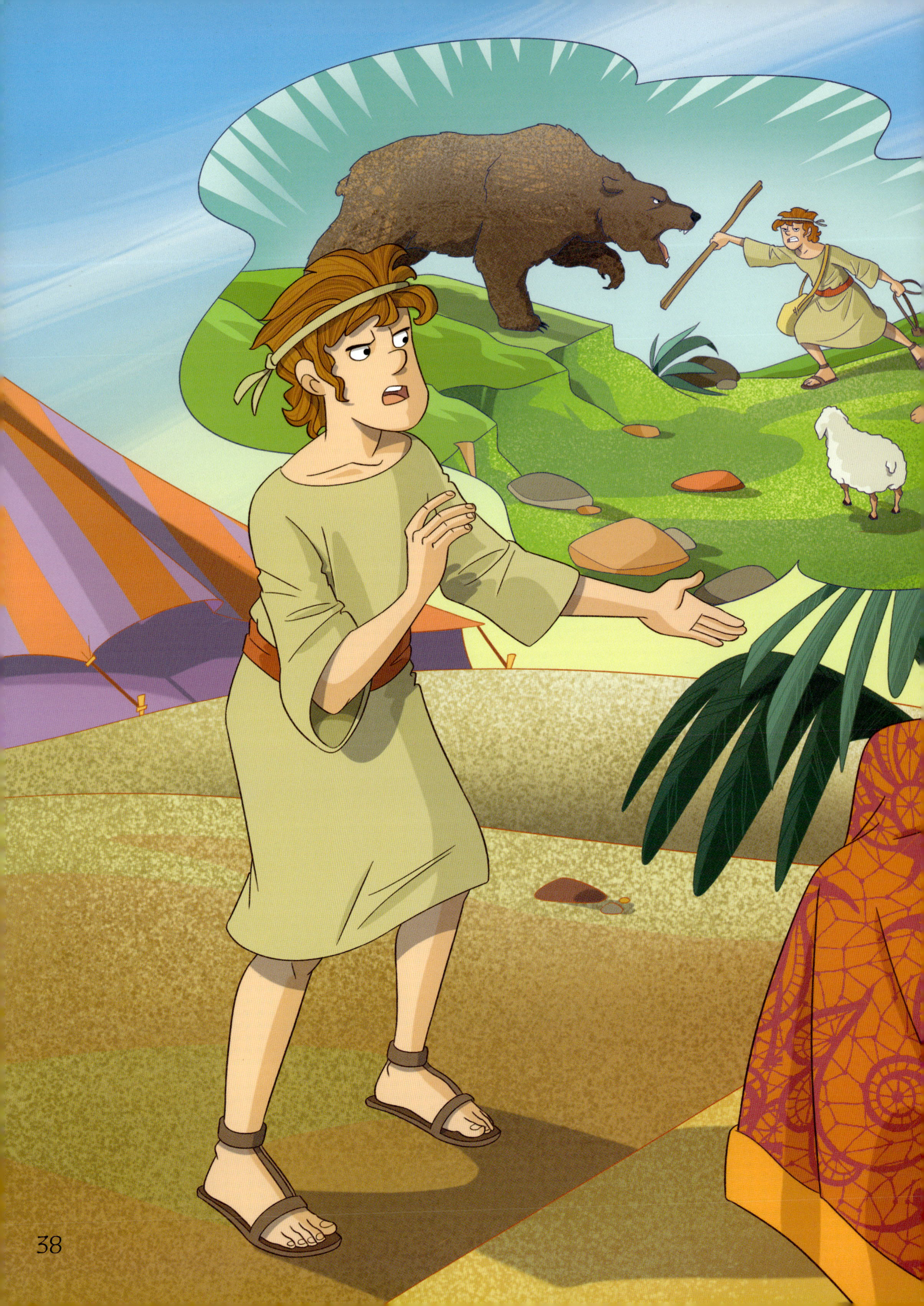

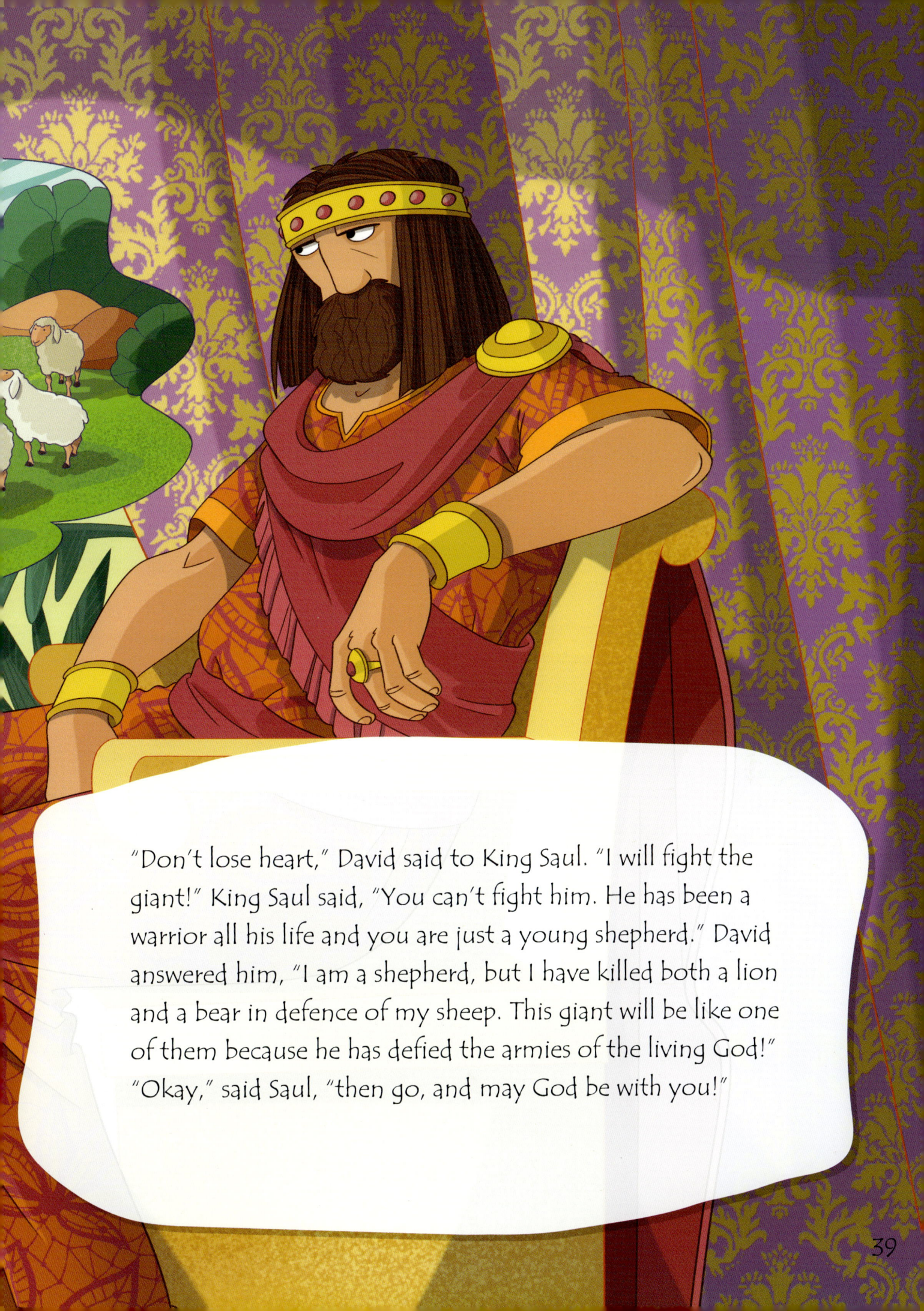

"Don't lose heart," David said to King Saul. "I will fight the giant!" King Saul said, "You can't fight him. He has been a warrior all his life and you are just a young shepherd." David answered him, "I am a shepherd, but I have killed both a lion and a bear in defence of my sheep. This giant will be like one of them because he has defied the armies of the living God!" "Okay," said Saul, "then go, and may God be with you!"

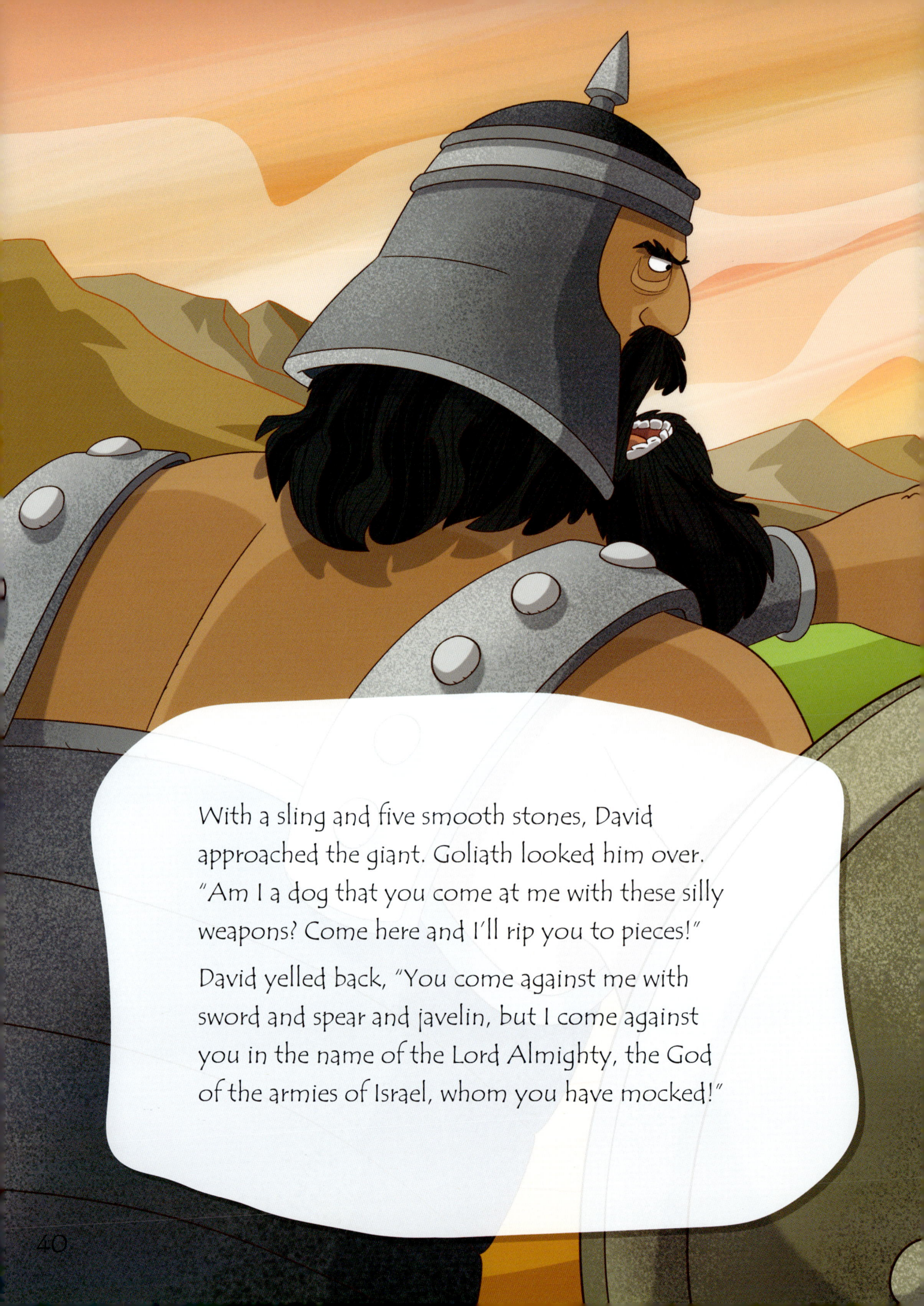

With a sling and five smooth stones, David approached the giant. Goliath looked him over. "Am I a dog that you come at me with these silly weapons? Come here and I'll rip you to pieces!"

David yelled back, "You come against me with sword and spear and javelin, but I come against you in the name of the Lord Almighty, the God of the armies of Israel, whom you have mocked!"

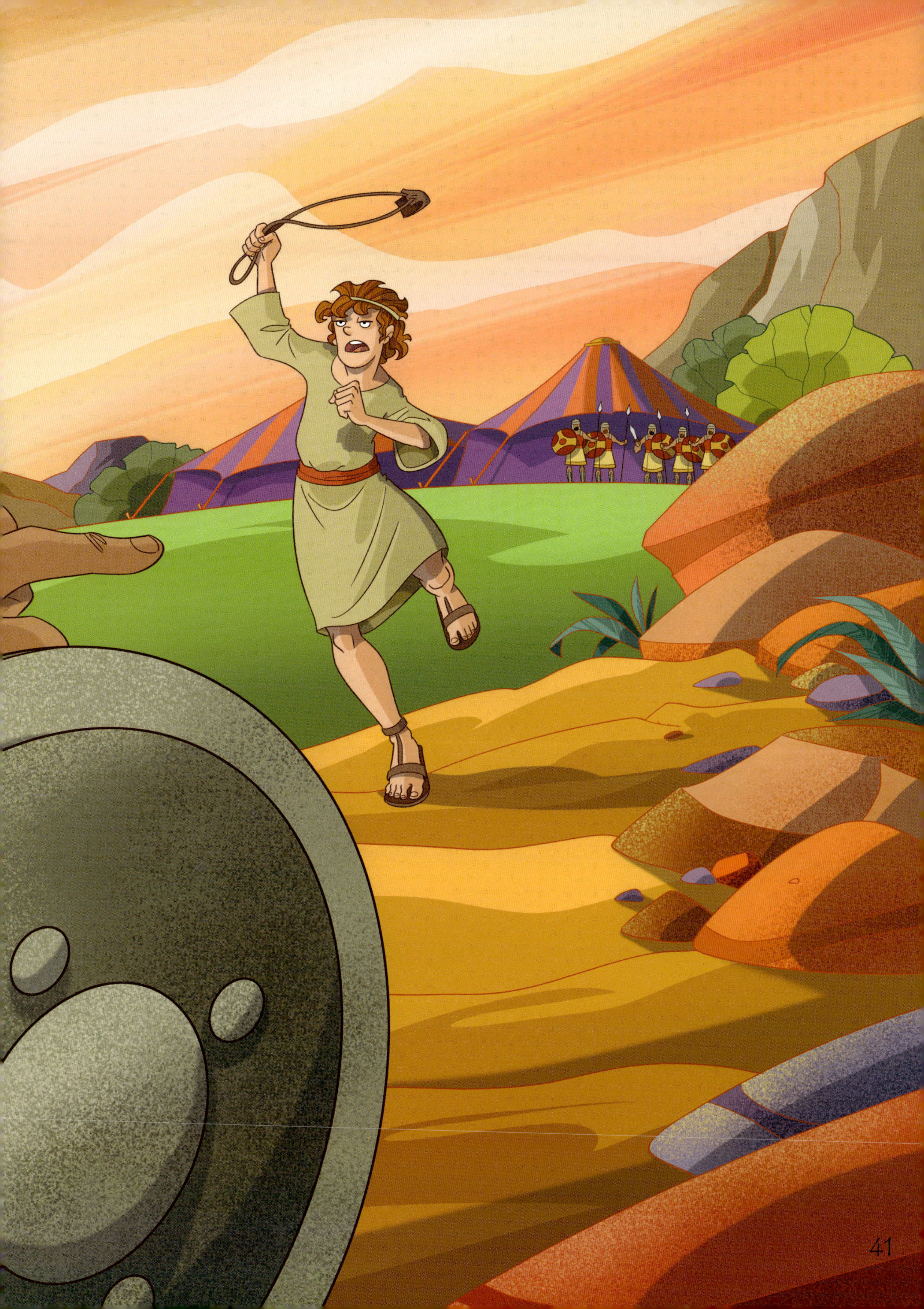

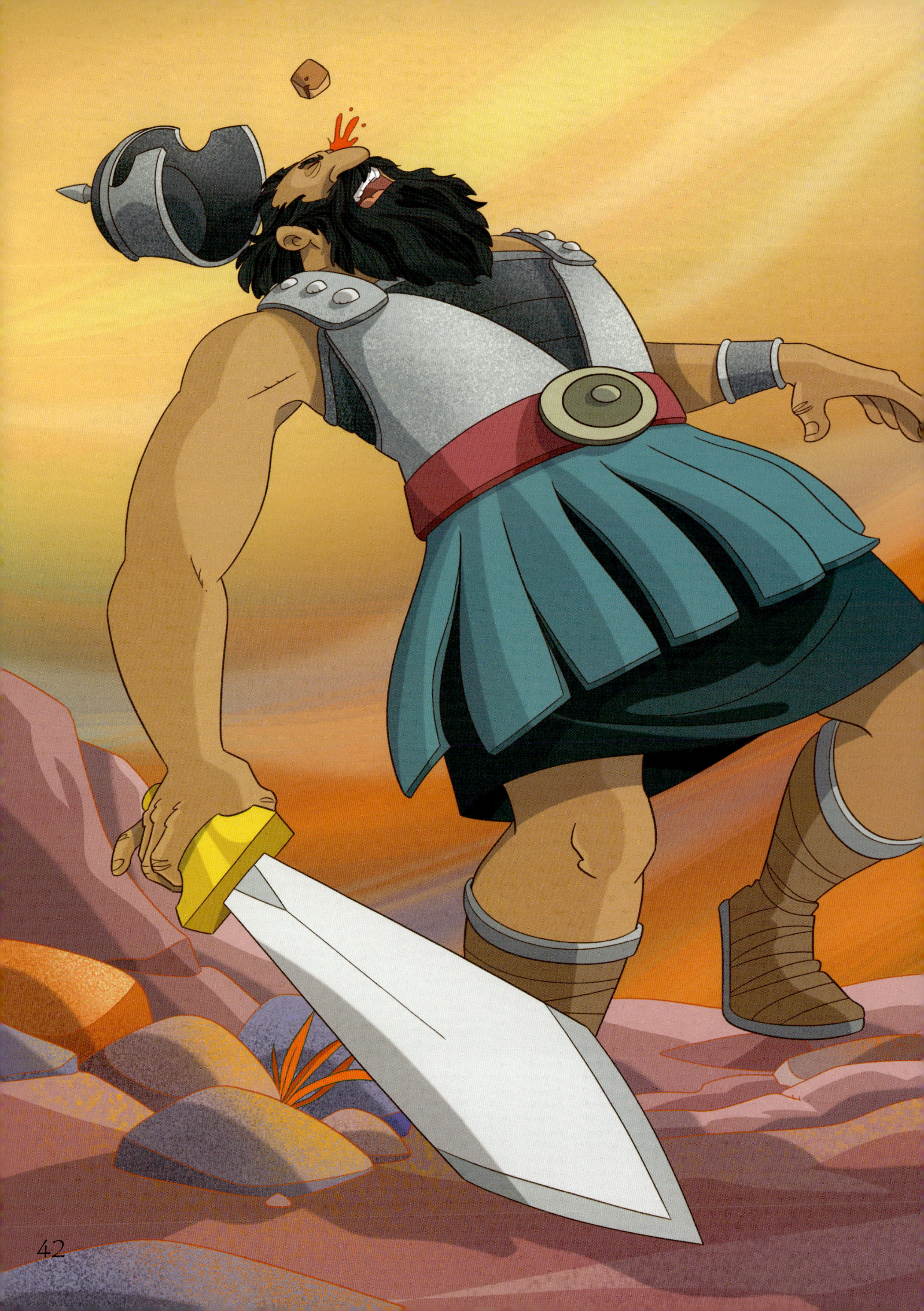

David took a stone out of his pouch, put it in his sling, and slung it at Goliath! *Thwack!* It hit him, right in the centre of his forehead! Goliath fell to the ground, dead.

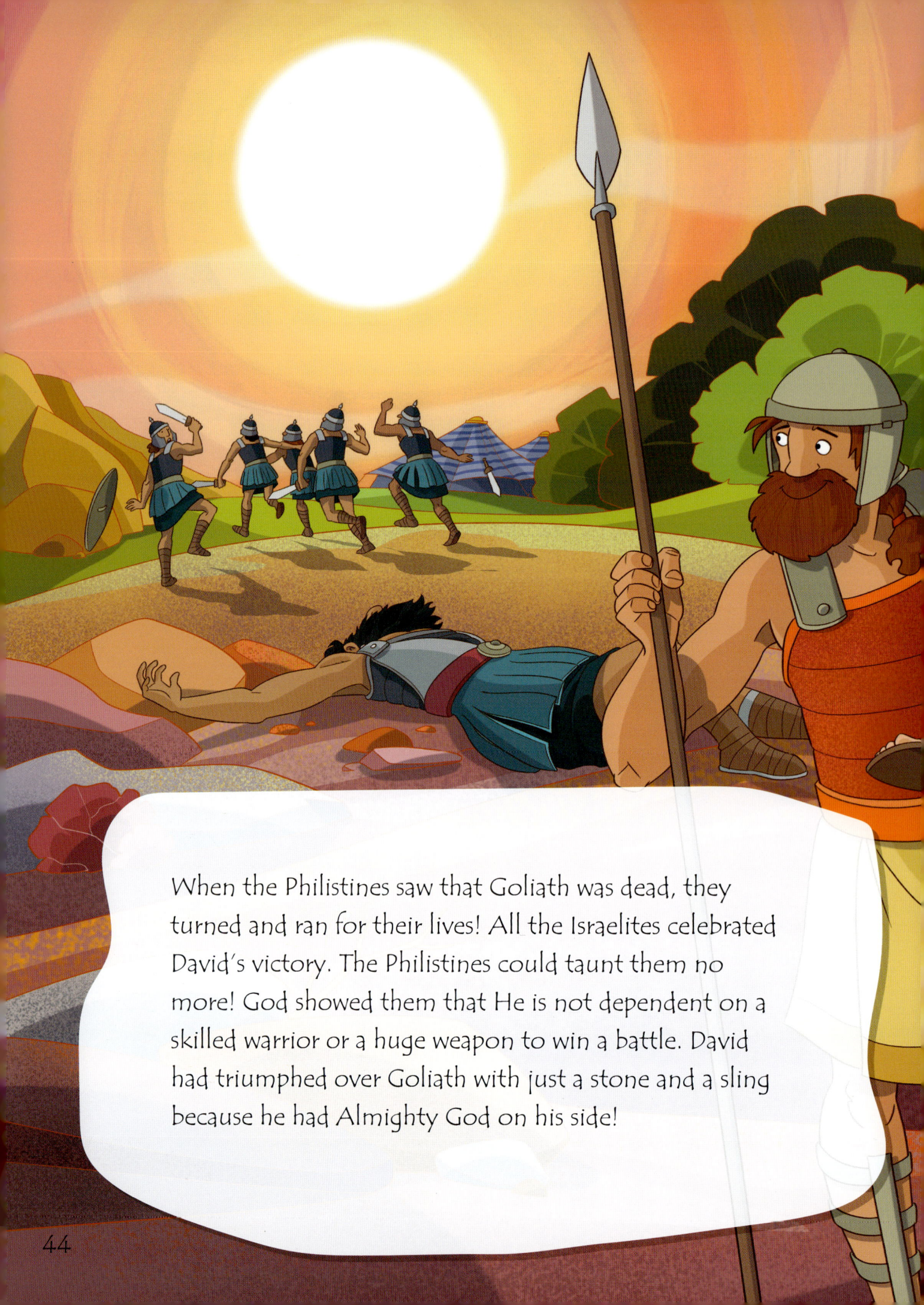

When the Philistines saw that Goliath was dead, they turned and ran for their lives! All the Israelites celebrated David's victory. The Philistines could taunt them no more! God showed them that He is not dependent on a skilled warrior or a huge weapon to win a battle. David had triumphed over Goliath with just a stone and a sling because he had Almighty God on his side!

45

The Foreign Girl Who Became a Brave Queen

Esther 1–10

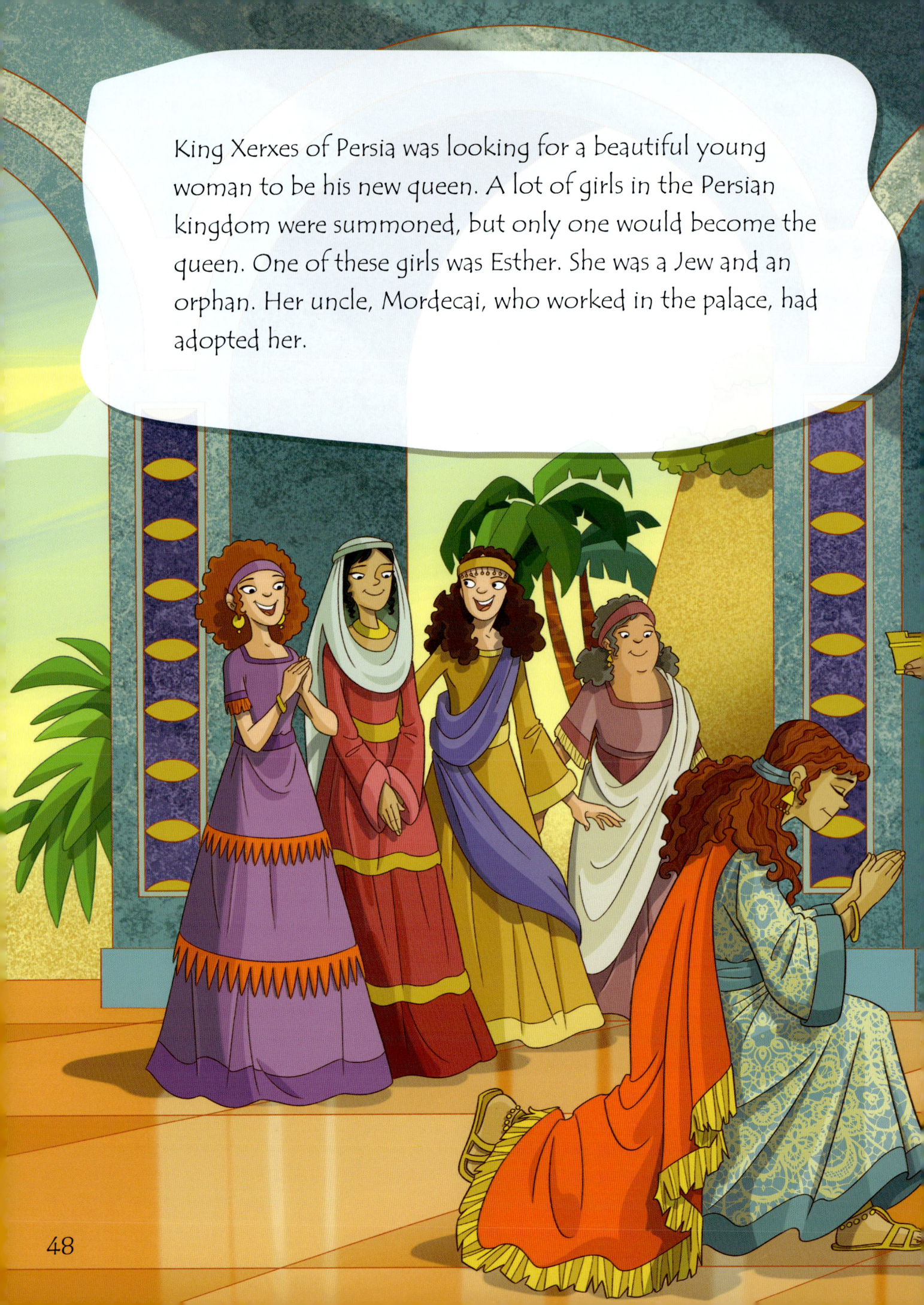

King Xerxes of Persia was looking for a beautiful young woman to be his new queen. A lot of girls in the Persian kingdom were summoned, but only one would become the queen. One of these girls was Esther. She was a Jew and an orphan. Her uncle, Mordecai, who worked in the palace, had adopted her.

After a full year of beauty treatments in the palace, each girl was presented to the king. The king immediately fell in love with Esther and chose her to be his wife, the new queen.

Some time later, the king made Haman, one of his nobles, more powerful than any other man in his entire kingdom. He commanded that everyone should bow down to Haman when they saw him. Mordecai, however, refused to bow down to Haman. "I'm a Jew and I can only bow down to the one true God!" Mordecai said. This made Haman furious, so he went to the king and said, "There is a group of people living in your kingdom who do not follow your orders."

"I think we should get rid of them all!" said Haman. The king didn't think much about who these people might be, but allowed Haman to do as he pleased.

When Esther's Uncle Mordecai found out, he dressed in sackcloth to show his sorrow and stood outside the palace crying. "Oh, Esther," Mordecai sobbed, "Haman has made a law that will cause all the Jews to be killed! Please go to the king and ask for help!" "But Uncle," said Esther, "I cannot just go to the king! If he doesn't first invite me to come, it might cost me my life to ask him for anything!"

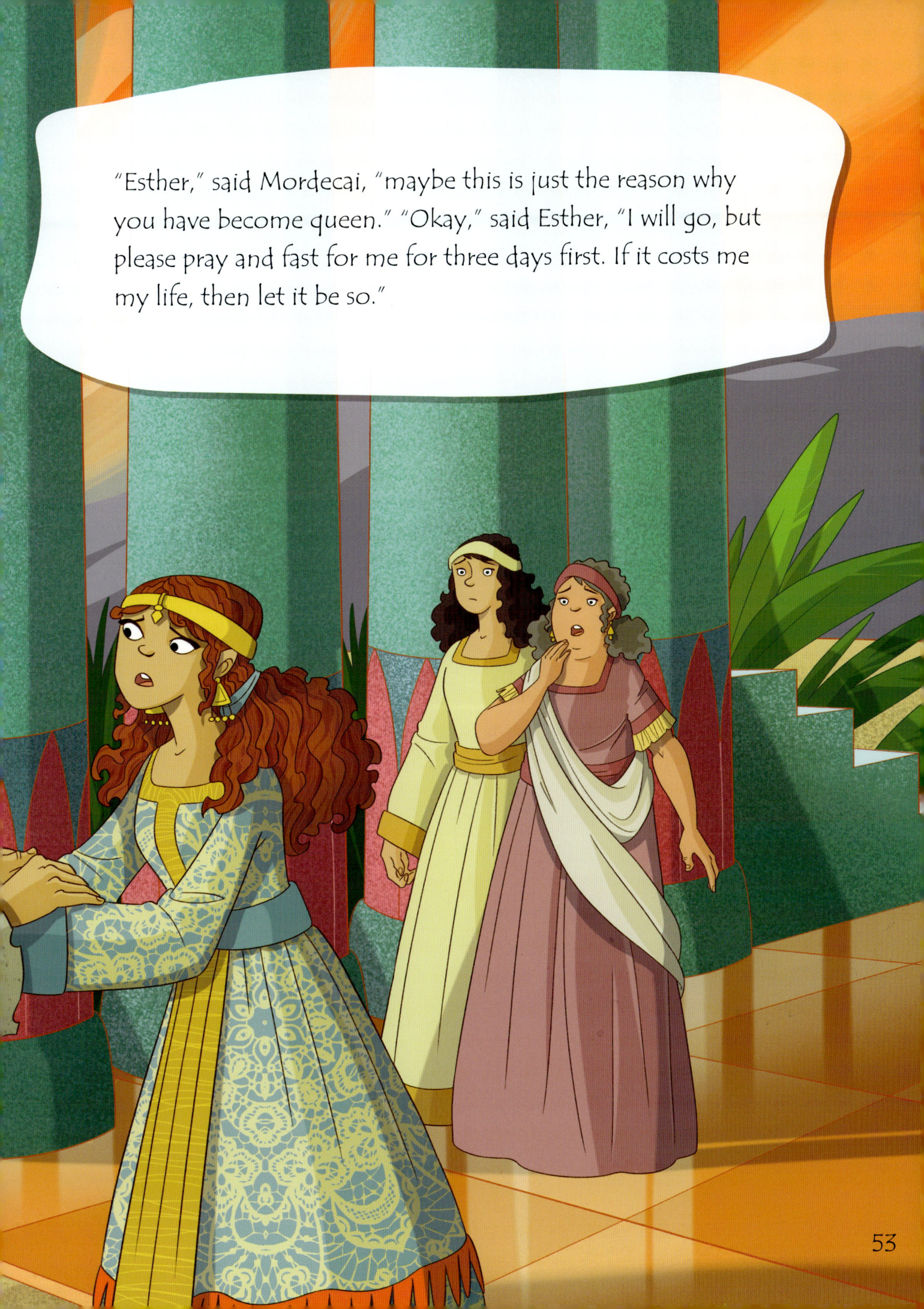

"Esther," said Mordecai, "maybe this is just the reason why you have become queen." "Okay," said Esther, "I will go, but please pray and fast for me for three days first. If it costs me my life, then let it be so."

After three days of fasting and praying, Esther put on her royal robes and stood in the entrance to the throne room. When the king saw her, to Esther's relief, he held out his gold sceptre and agreed to let her come to his throne.

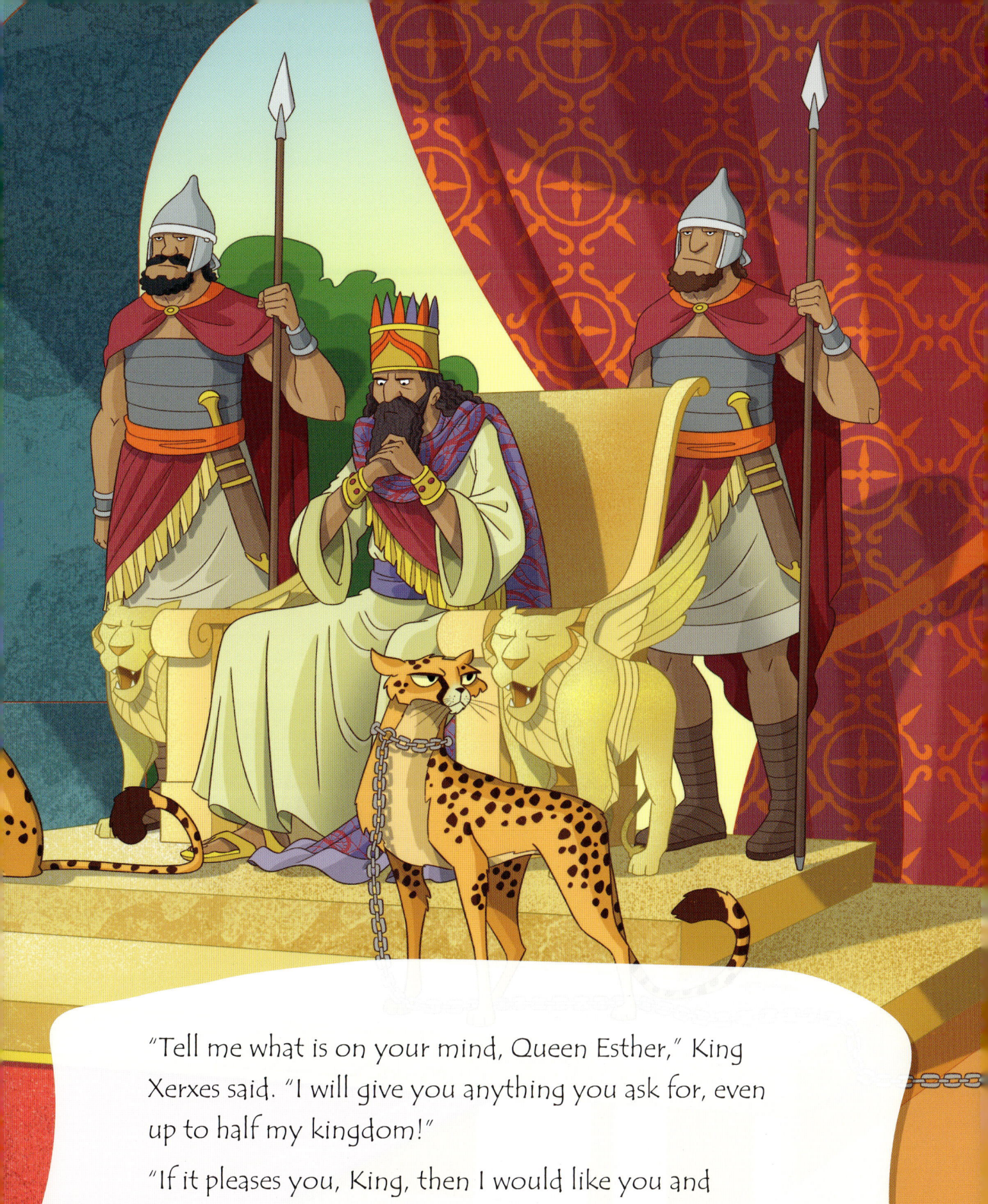

"Tell me what is on your mind, Queen Esther," King Xerxes said. "I will give you anything you ask for, even up to half my kingdom!"

"If it pleases you, King, then I would like you and Haman to come for a dinner that I myself will make for you," Esther answered.

Esther prepared food for a banquet, and, as they were eating, the king asked again, "Tell me what I can do for you, Queen Esther. I'll give you anything." Esther replied, "Oh, King. I only ask to live. For I and my people are in danger. A man has made a law that will have all the Jews killed."

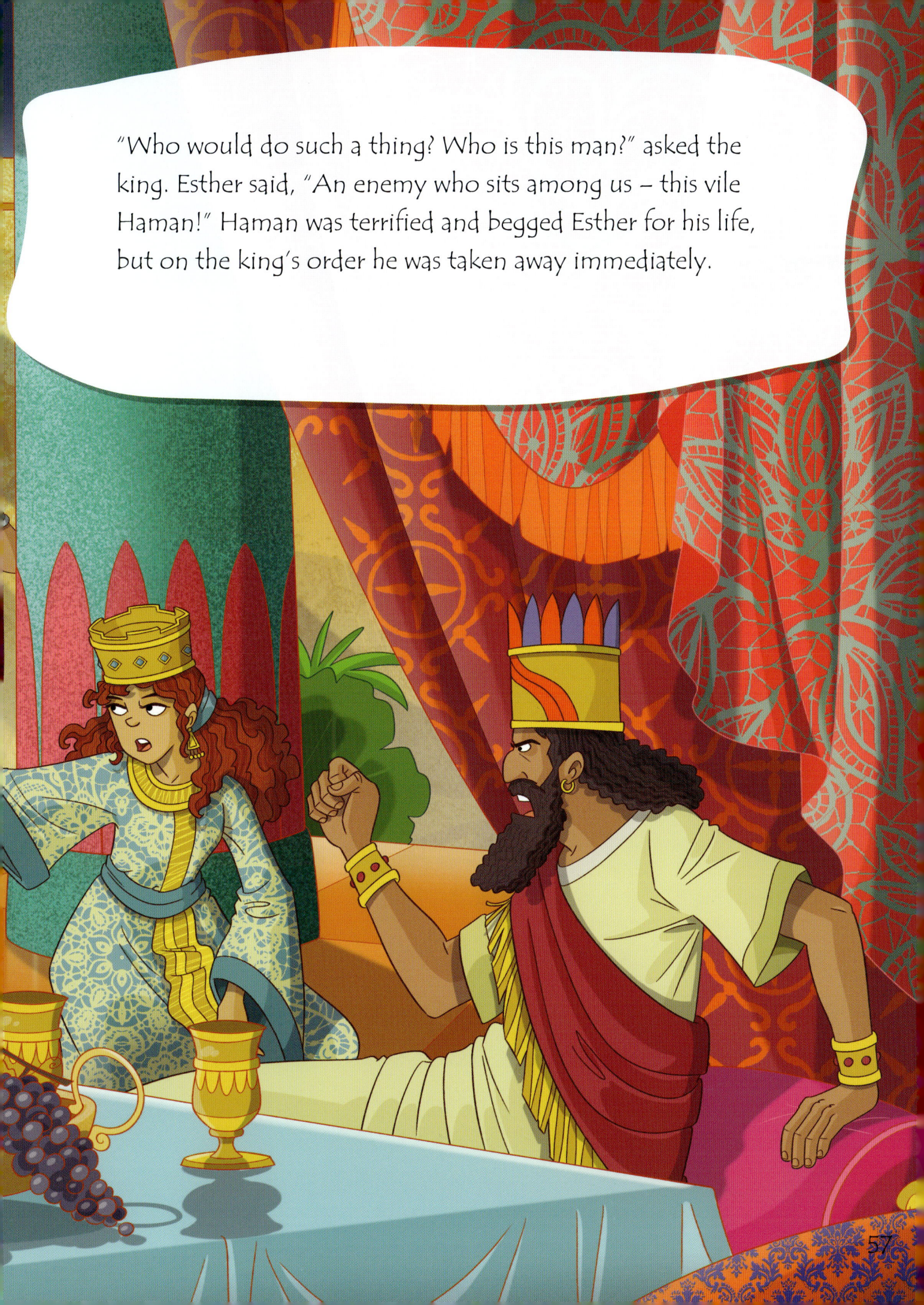

"Who would do such a thing? Who is this man?" asked the king. Esther said, "An enemy who sits among us – this vile Haman!" Haman was terrified and begged Esther for his life, but on the king's order he was taken away immediately.

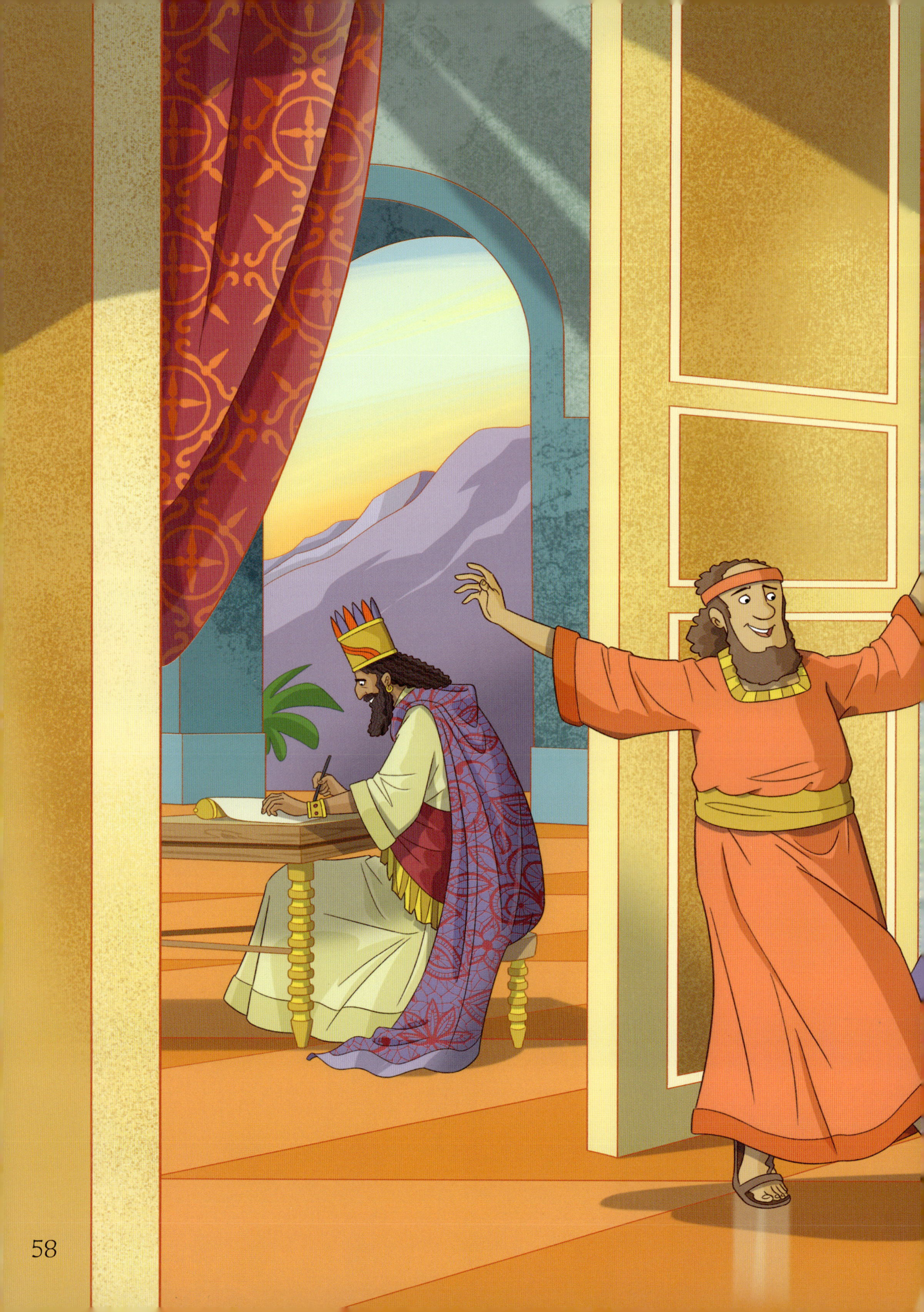

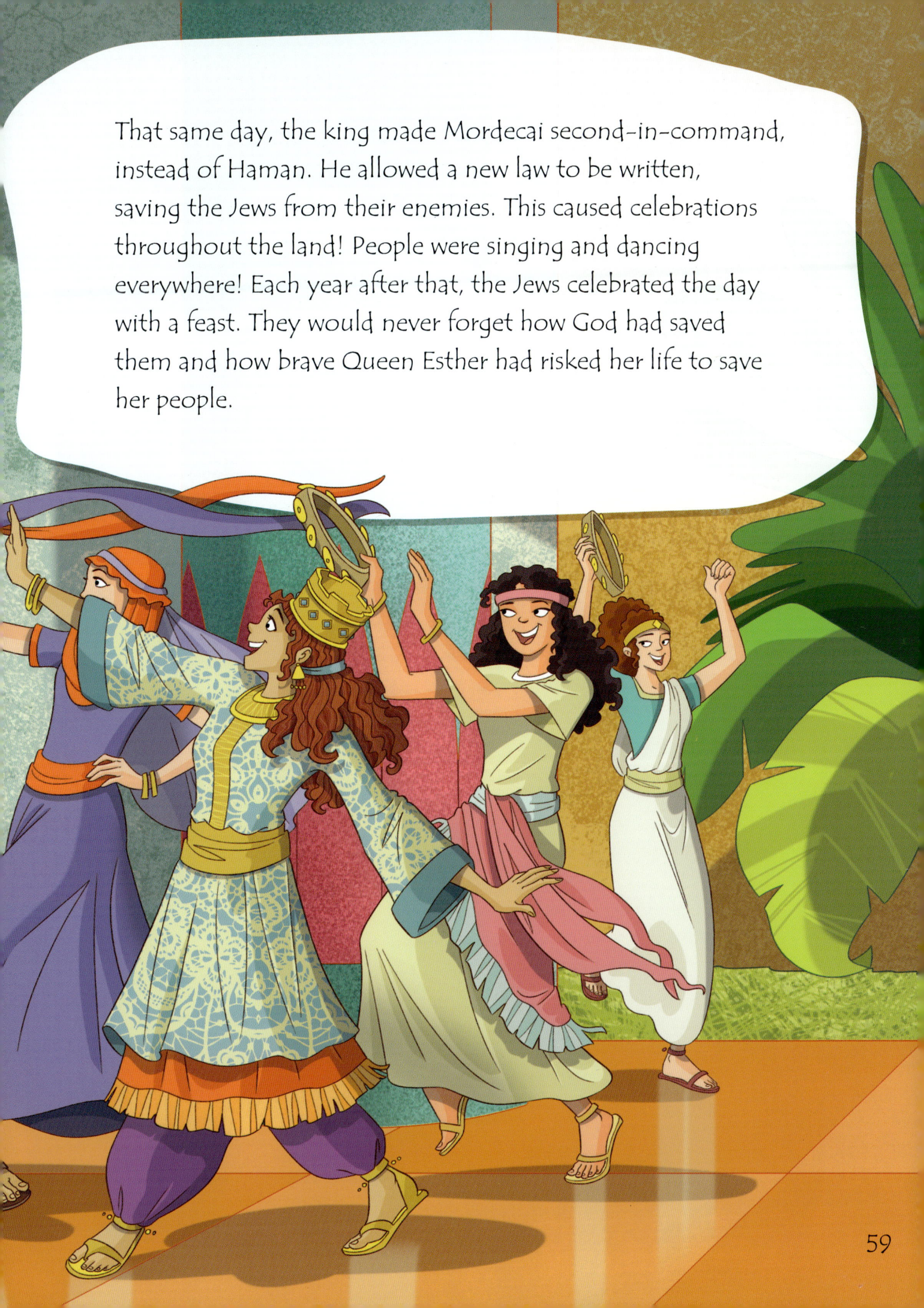

That same day, the king made Mordecai second-in-command, instead of Haman. He allowed a new law to be written, saving the Jews from their enemies. This caused celebrations throughout the land! People were singing and dancing everywhere! Each year after that, the Jews celebrated the day with a feast. They would never forget how God had saved them and how brave Queen Esther had risked her life to save her people.

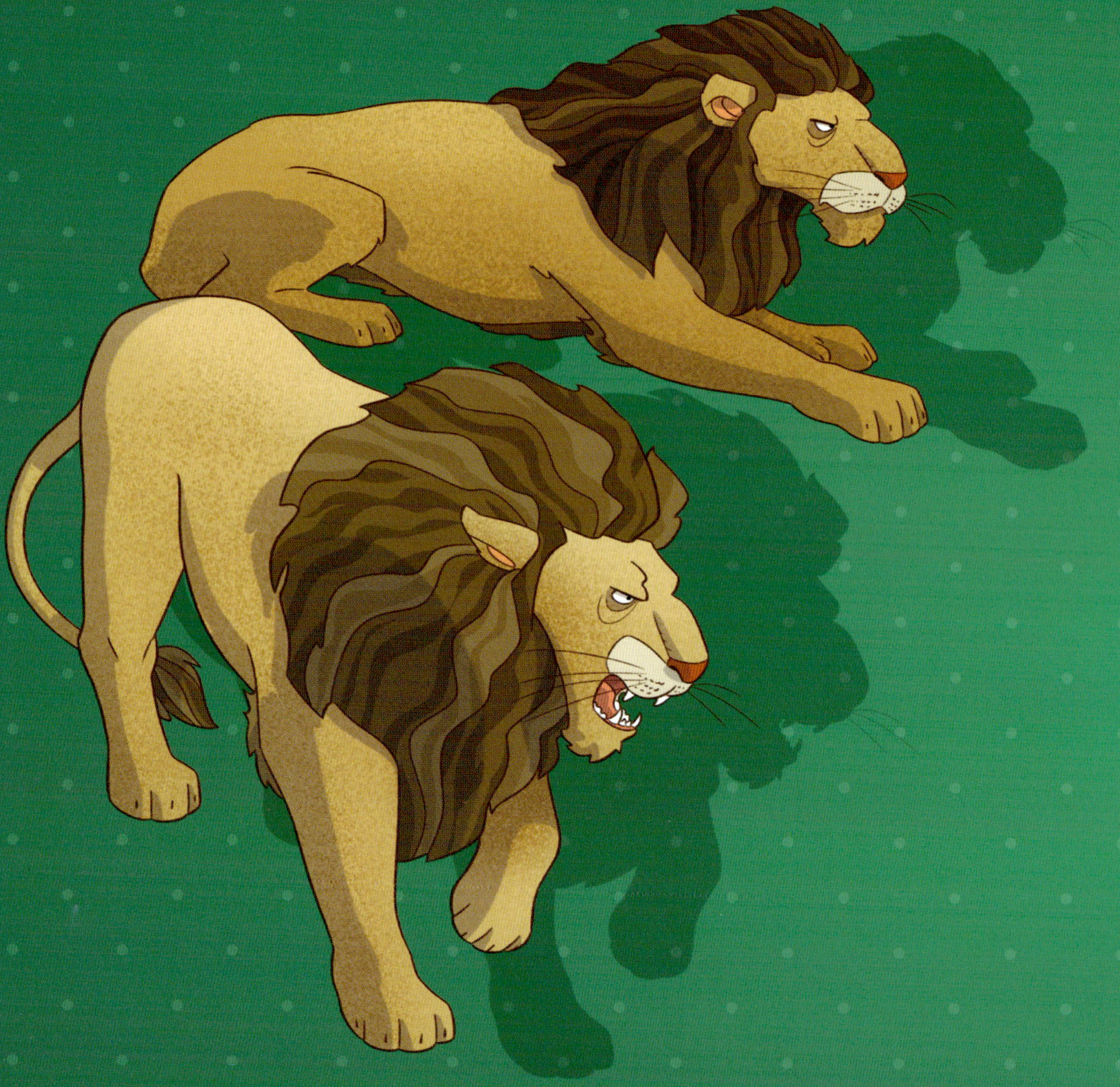

The Man Whose God Was Stronger than the Lions

Daniel 1 & 6

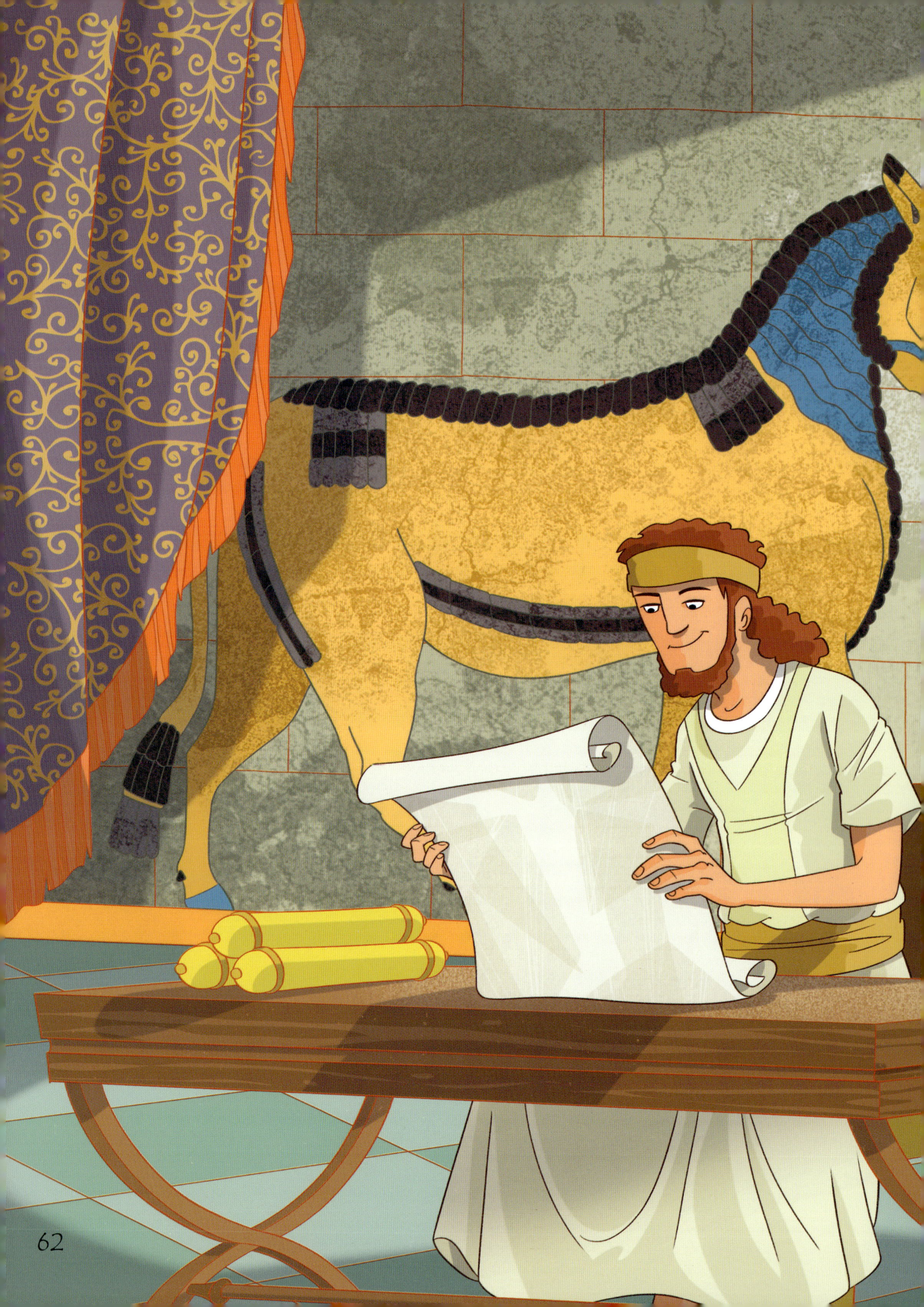

Daniel was a Jew, living in the kingdom of Babylon. He worked in the king's palace and God allowed him to do very well in his job. In fact, Daniel did so well that the king planned to put him second in charge over all the kingdom of Babylon.

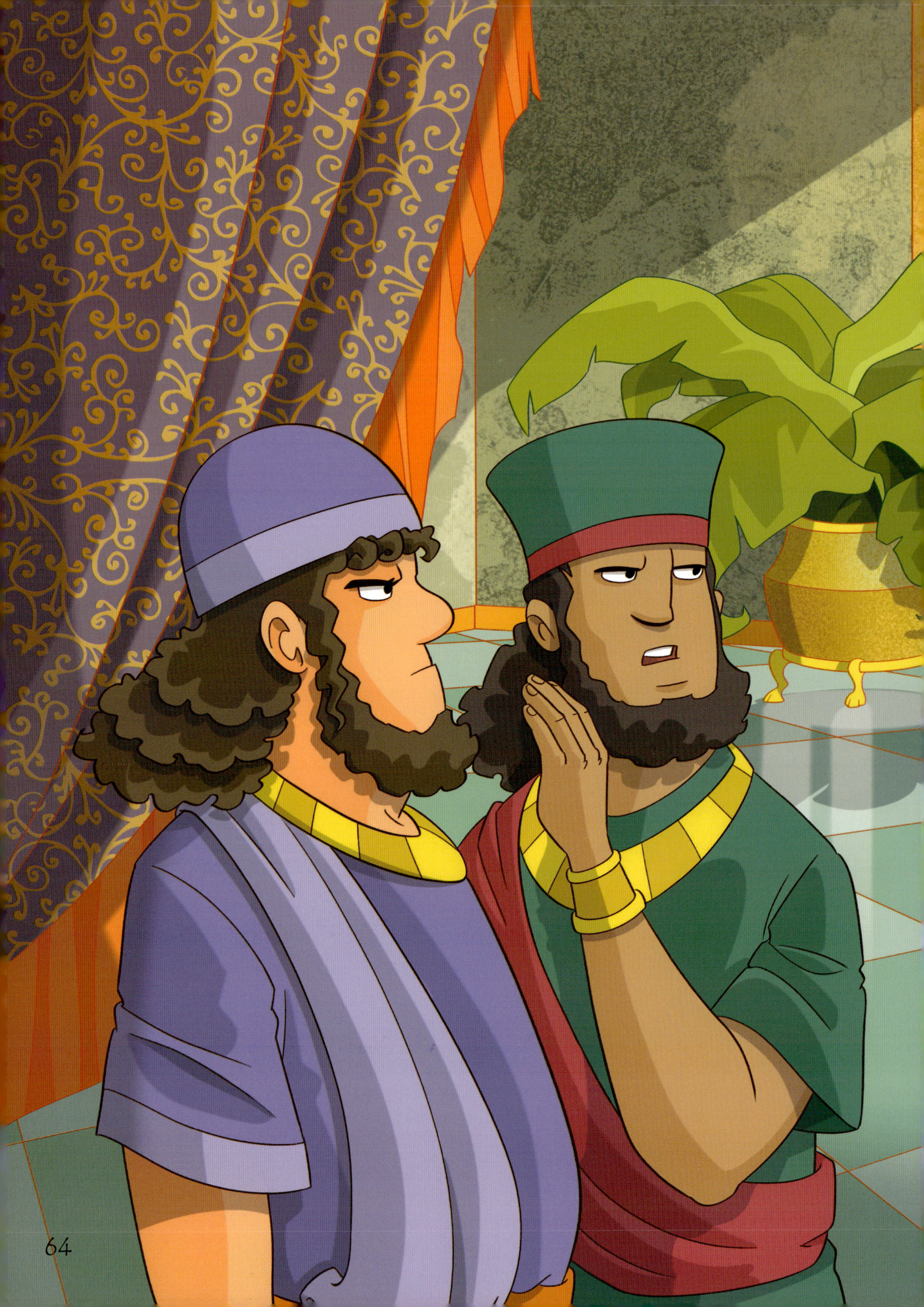

This made the other rulers jealous of him and they tried to find a way to prove to the king that Daniel was a failure. They knew Daniel prayed to God three times a day, so they tricked the king into making a new rule. If anyone was caught praying to anyone except the king in the next thirty days, they would be thrown into a den of lions!

66

Even though Daniel knew about the king's new rule, he also knew that it was wrong to pray to anyone but God. So, he continued giving thanks to God, three times a day, like he had done before.

The other men spied on Daniel, and when they saw him praying they went straight to the king to tattle on Daniel.

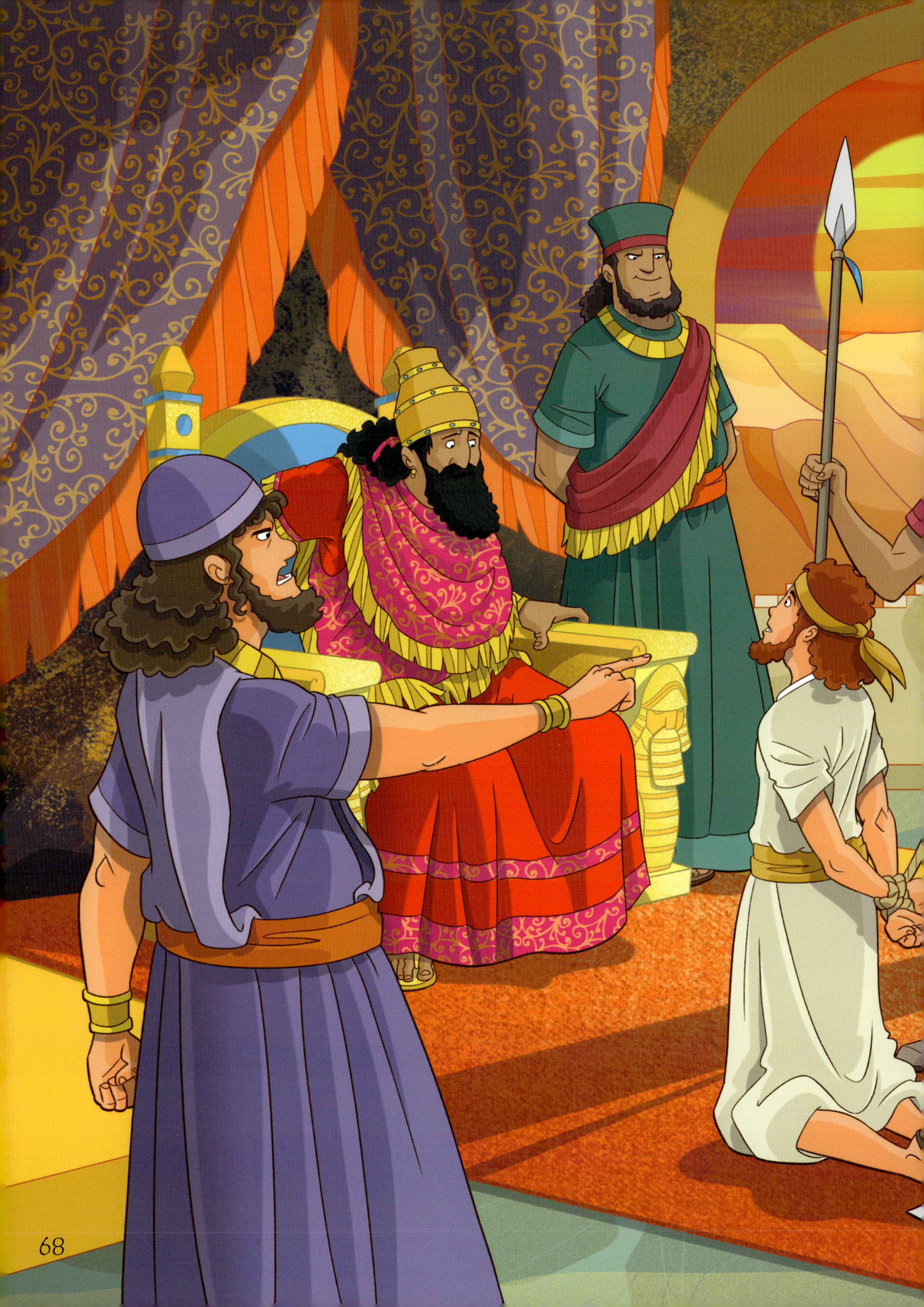

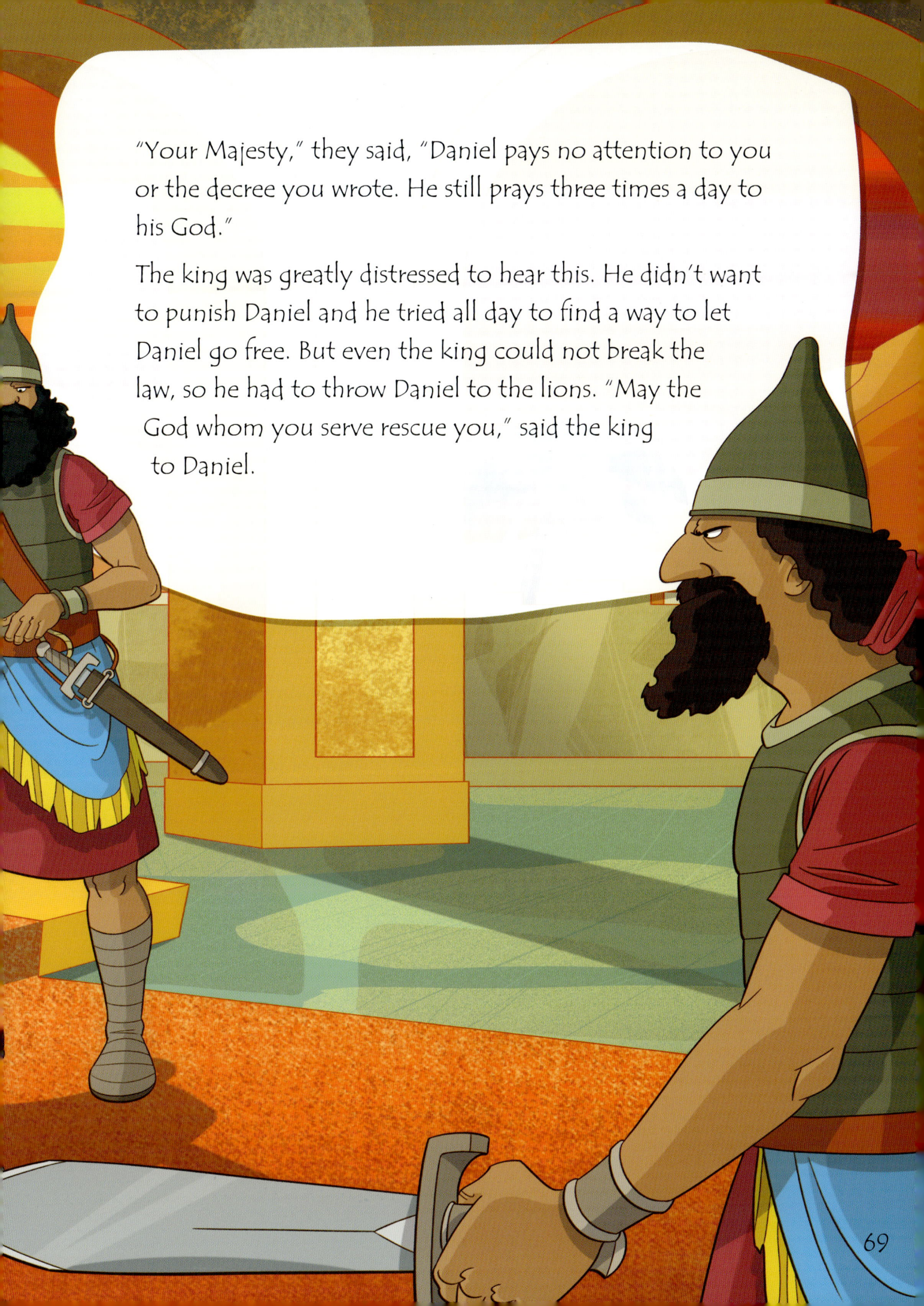

"Your Majesty," they said, "Daniel pays no attention to you or the decree you wrote. He still prays three times a day to his God."

The king was greatly distressed to hear this. He didn't want to punish Daniel and he tried all day to find a way to let Daniel go free. But even the king could not break the law, so he had to throw Daniel to the lions. "May the God whom you serve rescue you," said the king to Daniel.

As soon as the sun came up, the king got out of bed and hurried to the lions' den. "Daniel!" the king called out, fearing there would be no reply, "did your God rescue you from the lions?" Daniel shouted back, "Oh King! My God sent His angel to shut the lions' mouths, because in God's eyes I am innocent!"

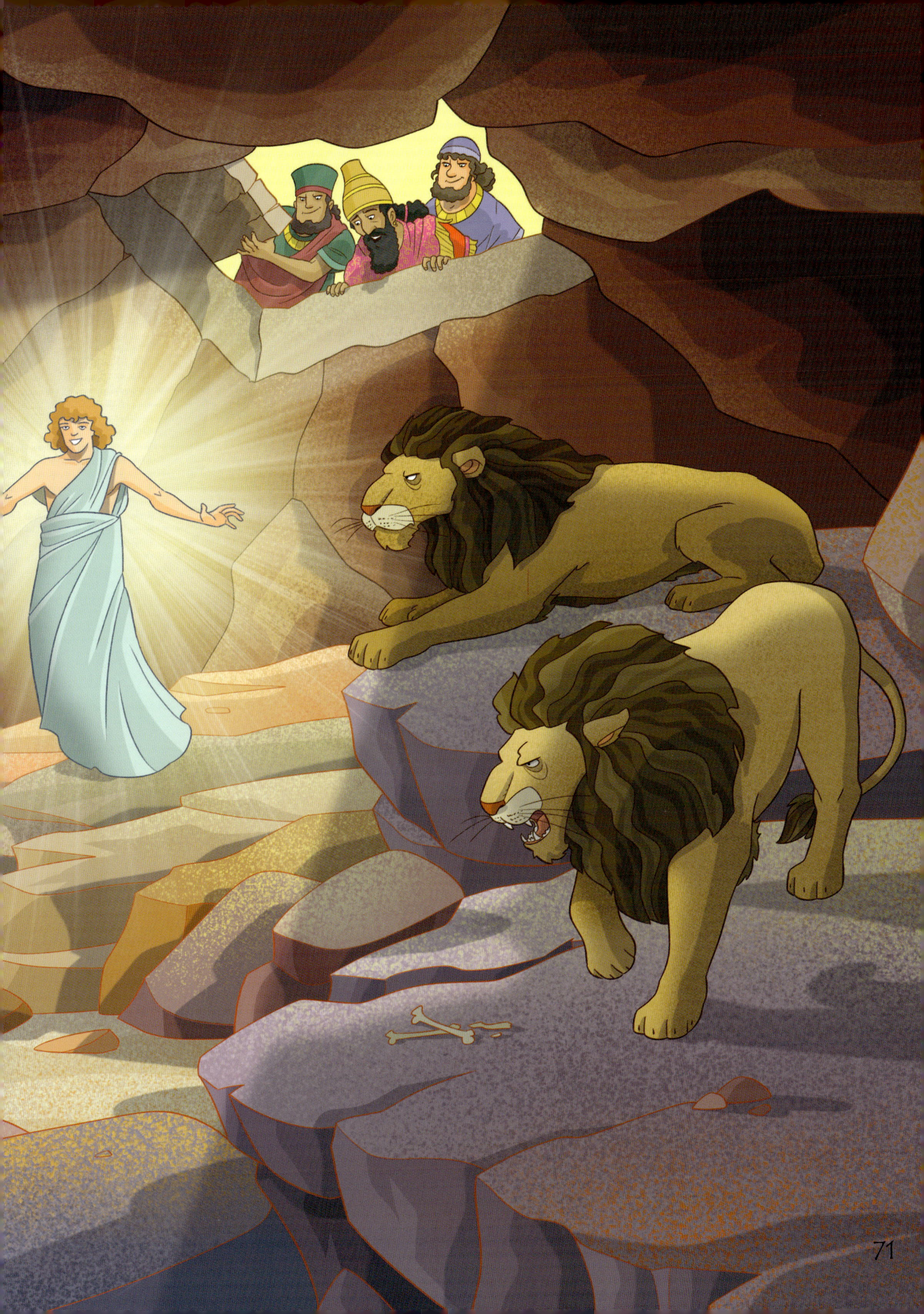

The king was overjoyed and ordered that the men who falsely accused Daniel be punished. Then he wrote a new law. "Everywhere in my kingdom," it said, "people must honour and respect Daniel's God. This God does wonders in heaven and on earth. Yes, He even saved Daniel from the powerful lions!"

73

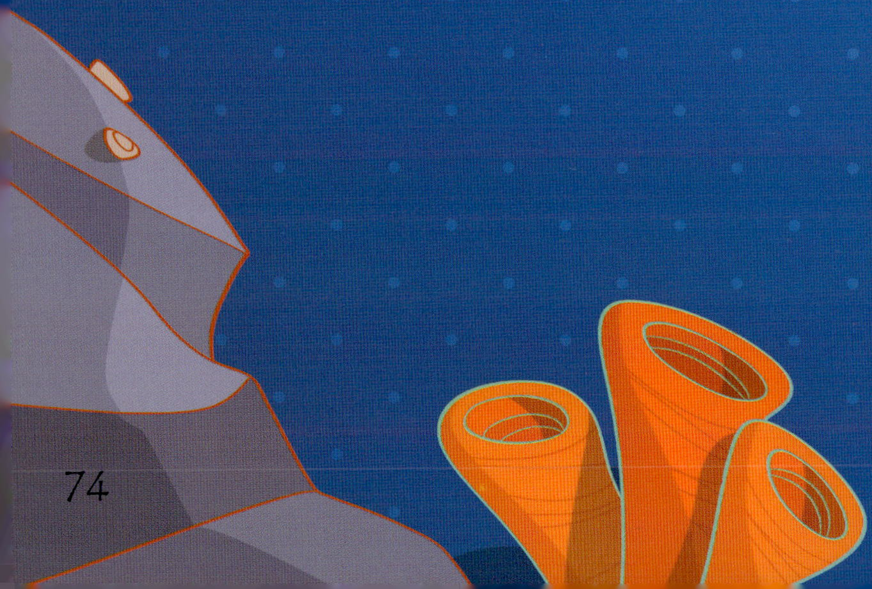

The Sulking Prophet Who Learned About God's Forgiveness

Jonah 1–4

One day, God told the prophet Jonah to go to the city of Nineveh and tell them to stop living in wickedness. However, Jonah didn't want to warn the Ninevites. He was a Jew and the Ninevites were so wicked that the Jews hated them. Instead, he decided to try to run away from God. He went down to the harbour to look for a ship heading to another city and got on it.

77

While the ship was at sea, God sent such a great storm that the ship almost broke apart. All the sailors were afraid. They cried out to their gods to save them and started throwing things overboard to lighten the ship. But Jonah said, "It is my fault that the storm is here. I'm running from God."

"Pick me up and throw me overboard, then everything will be calm again," Jonah said. The sailors had no choice but to follow what Jonah told them to do if they wanted to live through the storm. So, they threw him out of the ship and into the sea.

The minute Jonah sank into the water, the storm stopped and the sea grew calm again. When the sailors saw this, they were amazed and worshipped Jonah's God. As Jonah sank to the bottom of the sea, God allowed a huge fish to swallow him. In the belly of the fish, Jonah prayed, "Please forgive me, God. Give me another chance to do what is right."

81

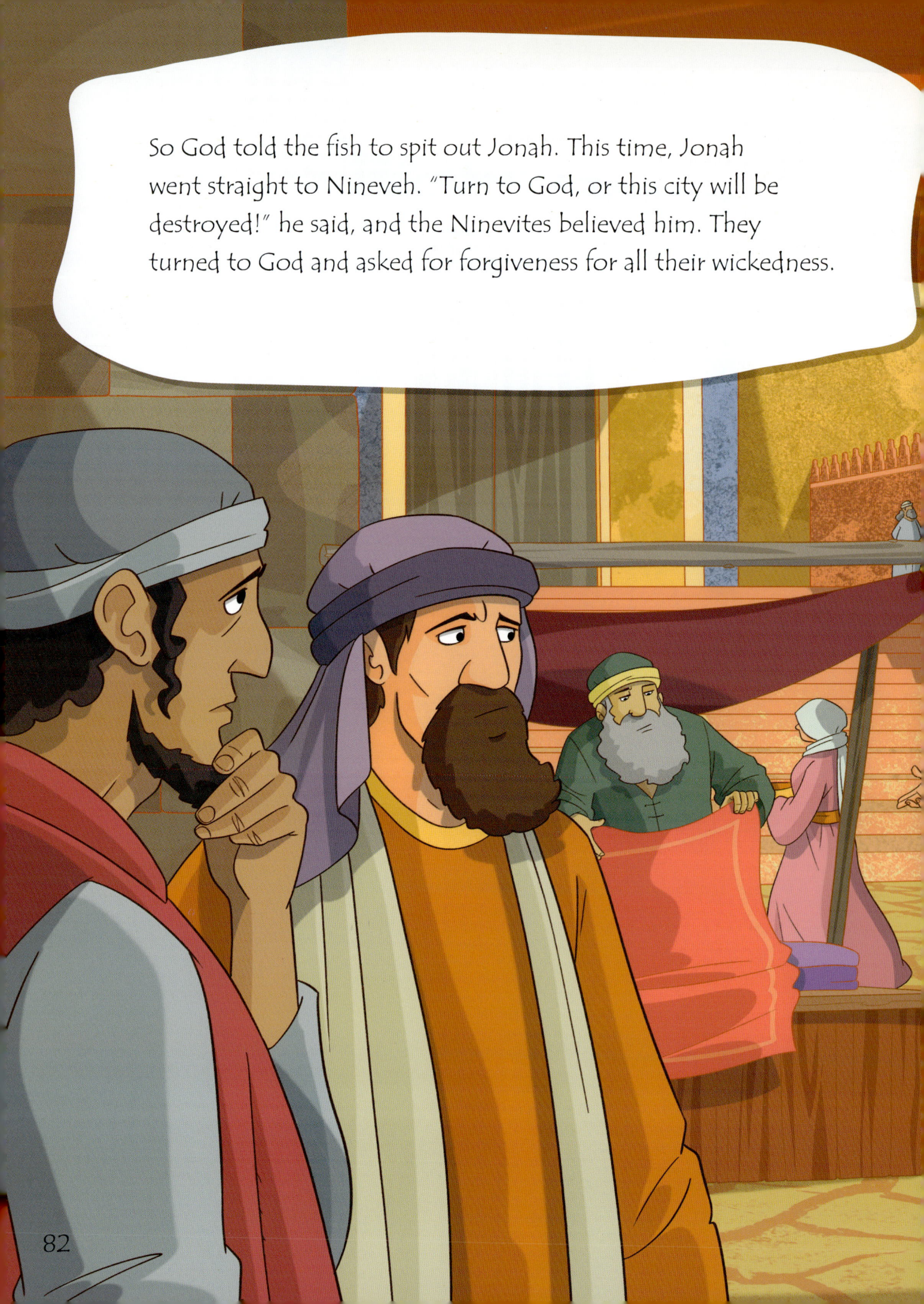

So God told the fish to spit out Jonah. This time, Jonah went straight to Nineveh. "Turn to God, or this city will be destroyed!" he said, and the Ninevites believed him. They turned to God and asked for forgiveness for all their wickedness.

83

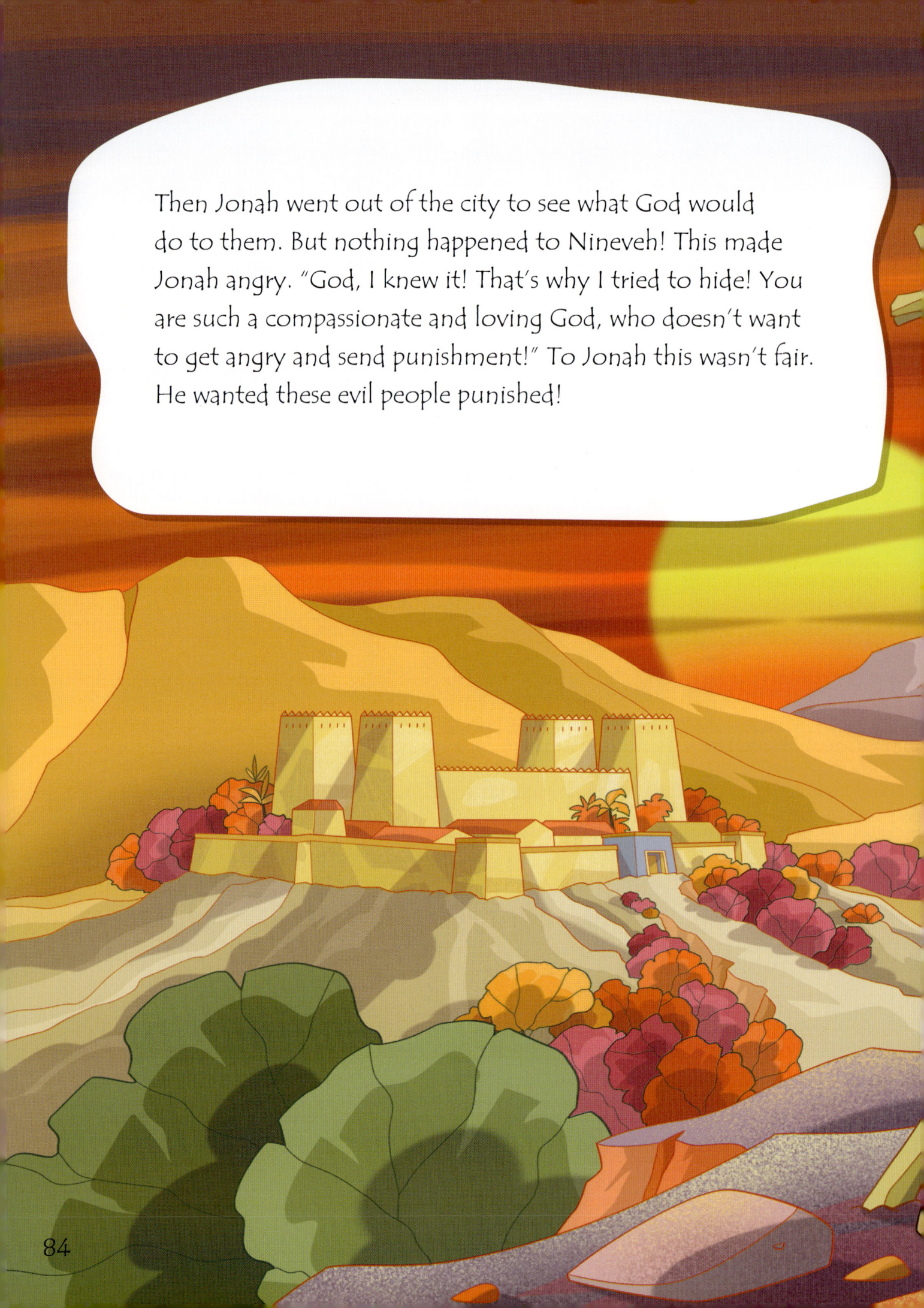

Then Jonah went out of the city to see what God would do to them. But nothing happened to Nineveh! This made Jonah angry. "God, I knew it! That's why I tried to hide! You are such a compassionate and loving God, who doesn't want to get angry and send punishment!" To Jonah this wasn't fair. He wanted these evil people punished!

85

86

God answered Jonah, "It isn't right for you to be angry. Why should I not be concerned about the one hundred and twenty thousand people in Nineveh? I have seen how sorry they all are and I have forgiven them of their wickedness."

The Son Who Thought He Knew Better

Luke 15:11-32

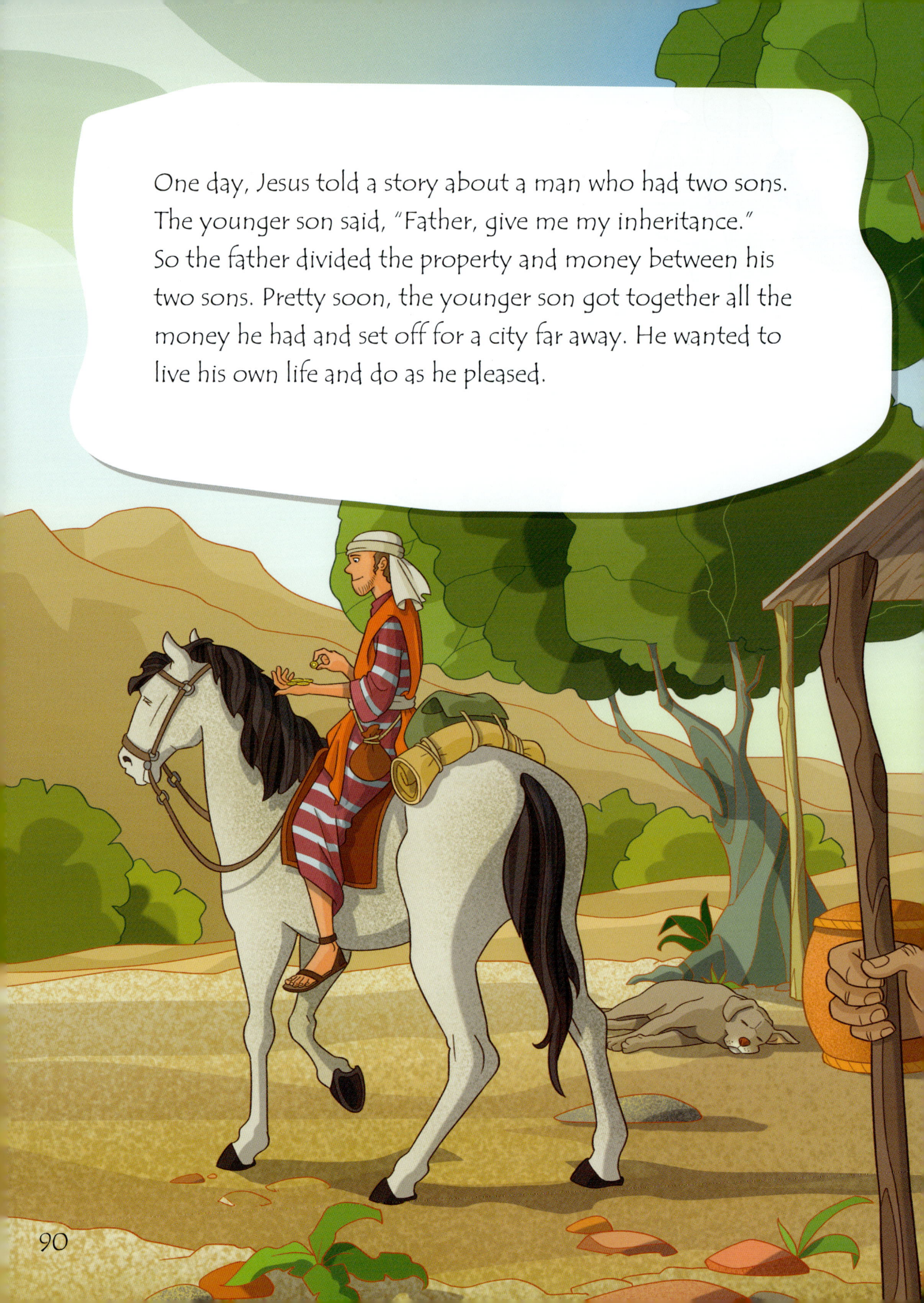

One day, Jesus told a story about a man who had two sons. The younger son said, "Father, give me my inheritance." So the father divided the property and money between his two sons. Pretty soon, the younger son got together all the money he had and set off for a city far away. He wanted to live his own life and do as he pleased.

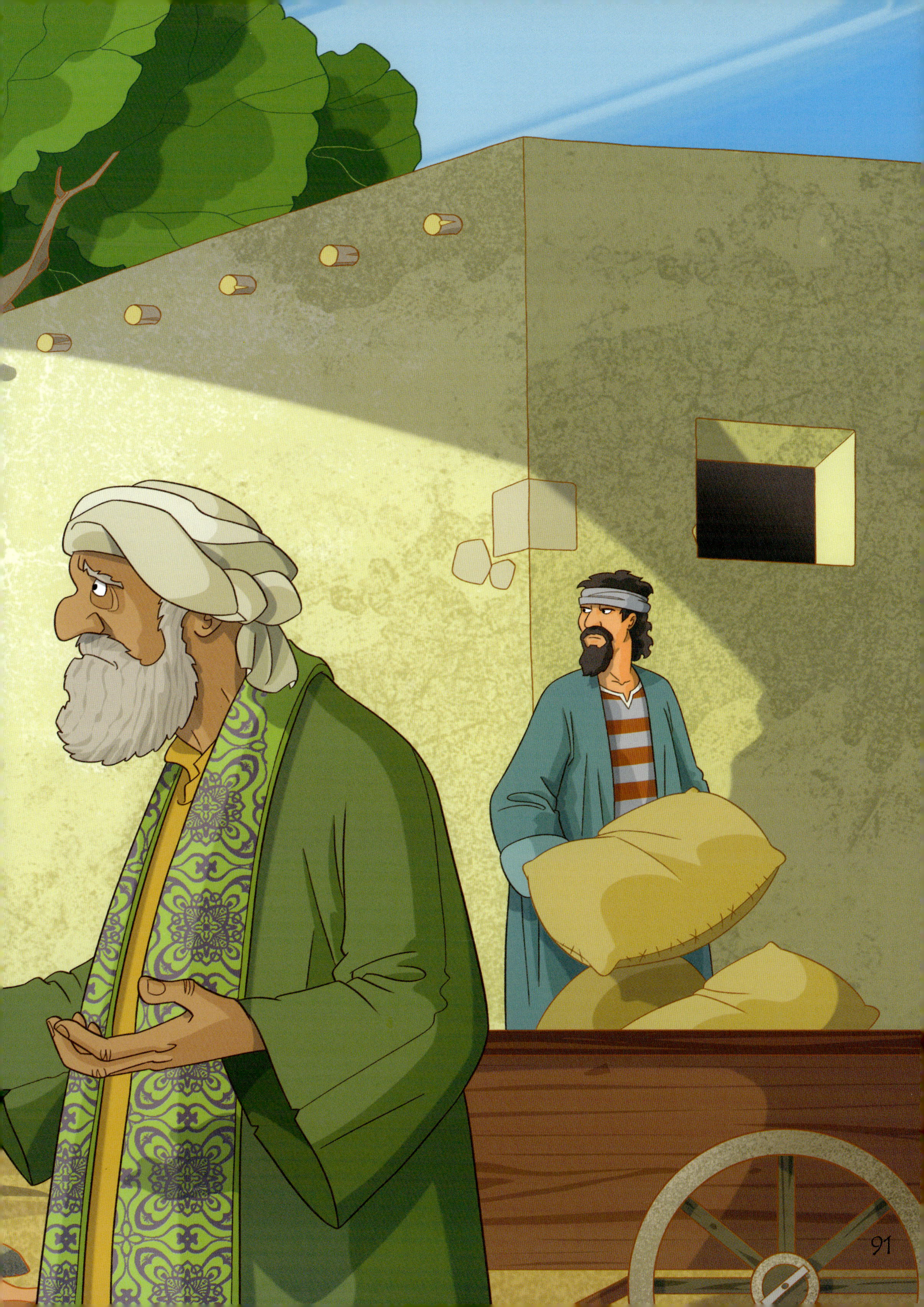

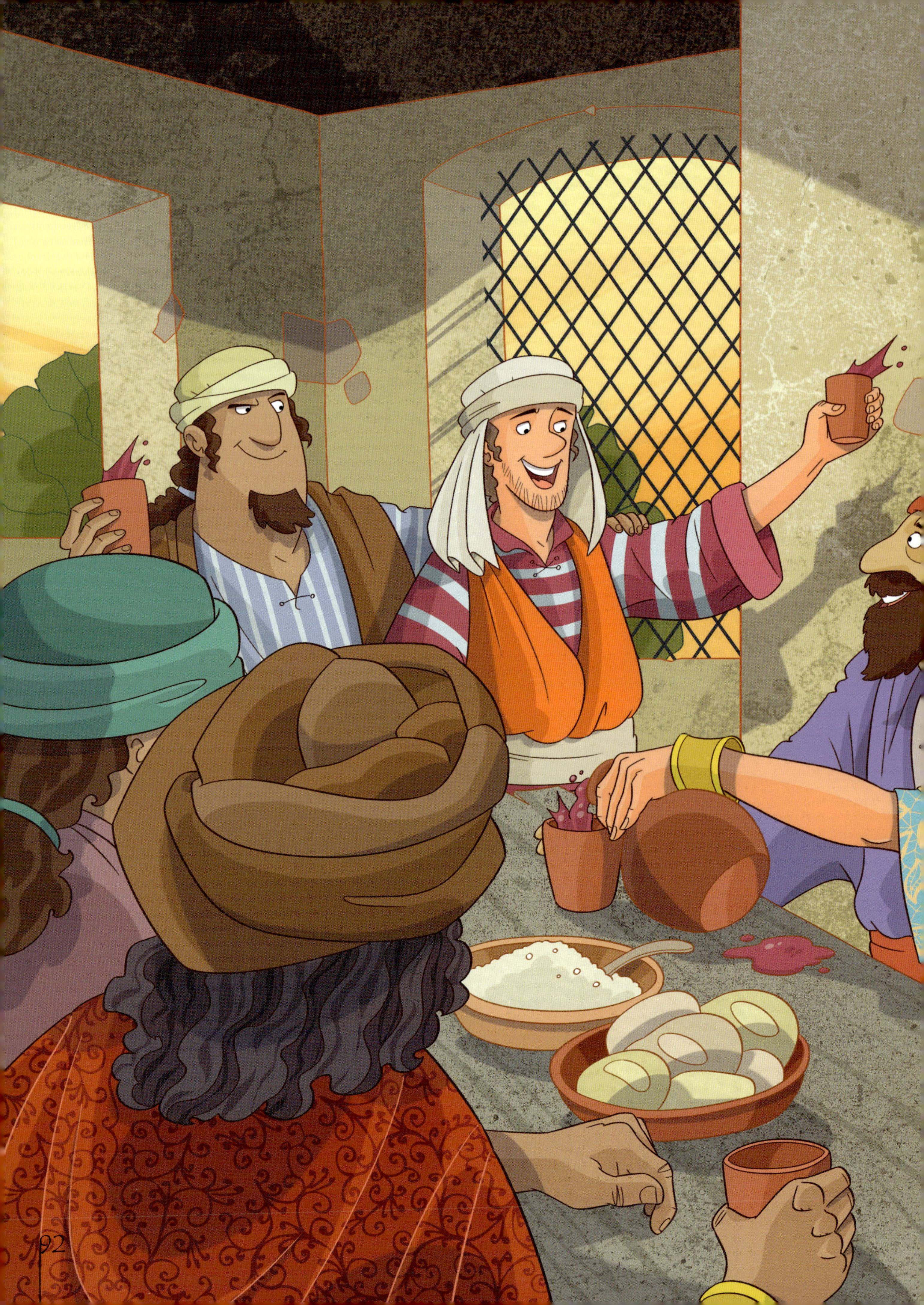

The young man spent the money his father had given him on wild living. Everything he wanted, he bought. Everything he wanted to do, he did. But after a while his money ran out. Then, when a famine came over the country and the young man had no money left, he was suddenly in great trouble.

93

He found a farmer who gave him a job feeding the pigs in his field. The job did not pay much. In fact, the young man was still so poor that he was hungry enough to eat the pigs' food! At that point, he came to his senses and said to himself, "How many of my father's servants have more than enough food, and here I am, starving to death! I will go back to my father and ask if he will take me in as one of his servants." So he left and started off towards home.

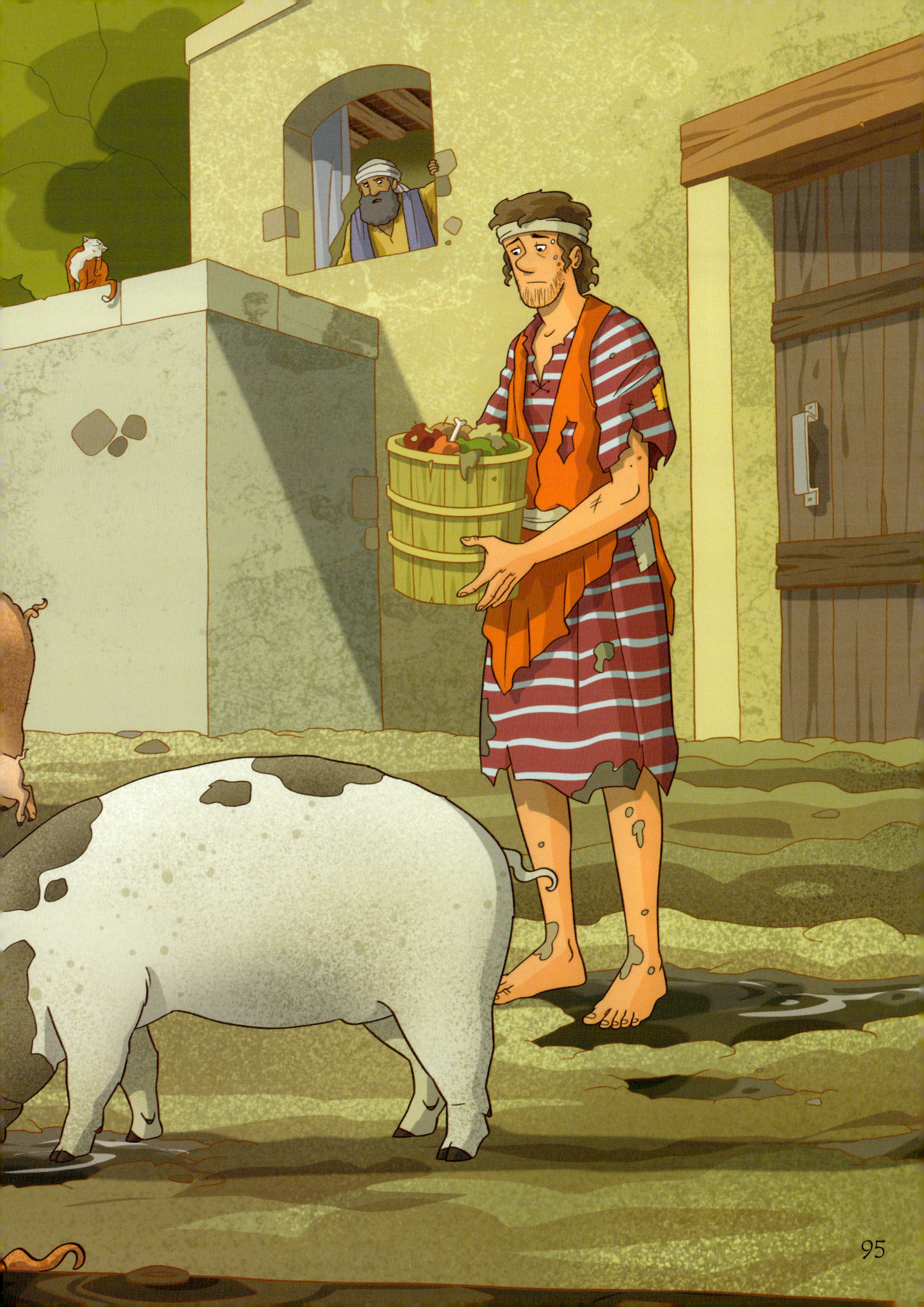

As he walked towards his father's house, the young son saw his father running to meet him. The father had seen him from afar and was filled with compassion for him. When he reached his son, he threw his arms around him and hugged him. "Father," said the son, "I have sinned against God and you and I am no longer worthy to be your son."

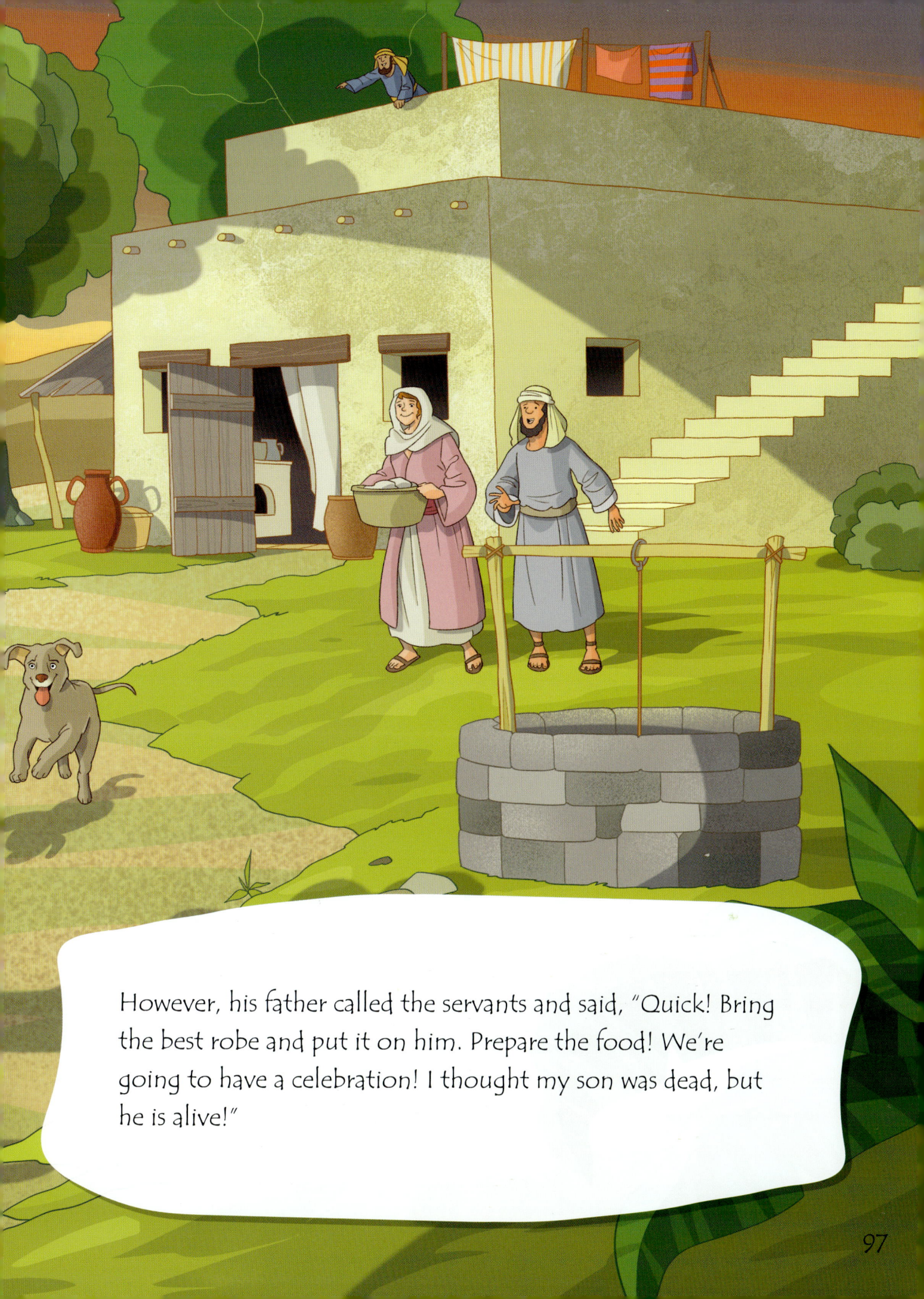

However, his father called the servants and said, "Quick! Bring the best robe and put it on him. Prepare the food! We're going to have a celebration! I thought my son was dead, but he is alive!"

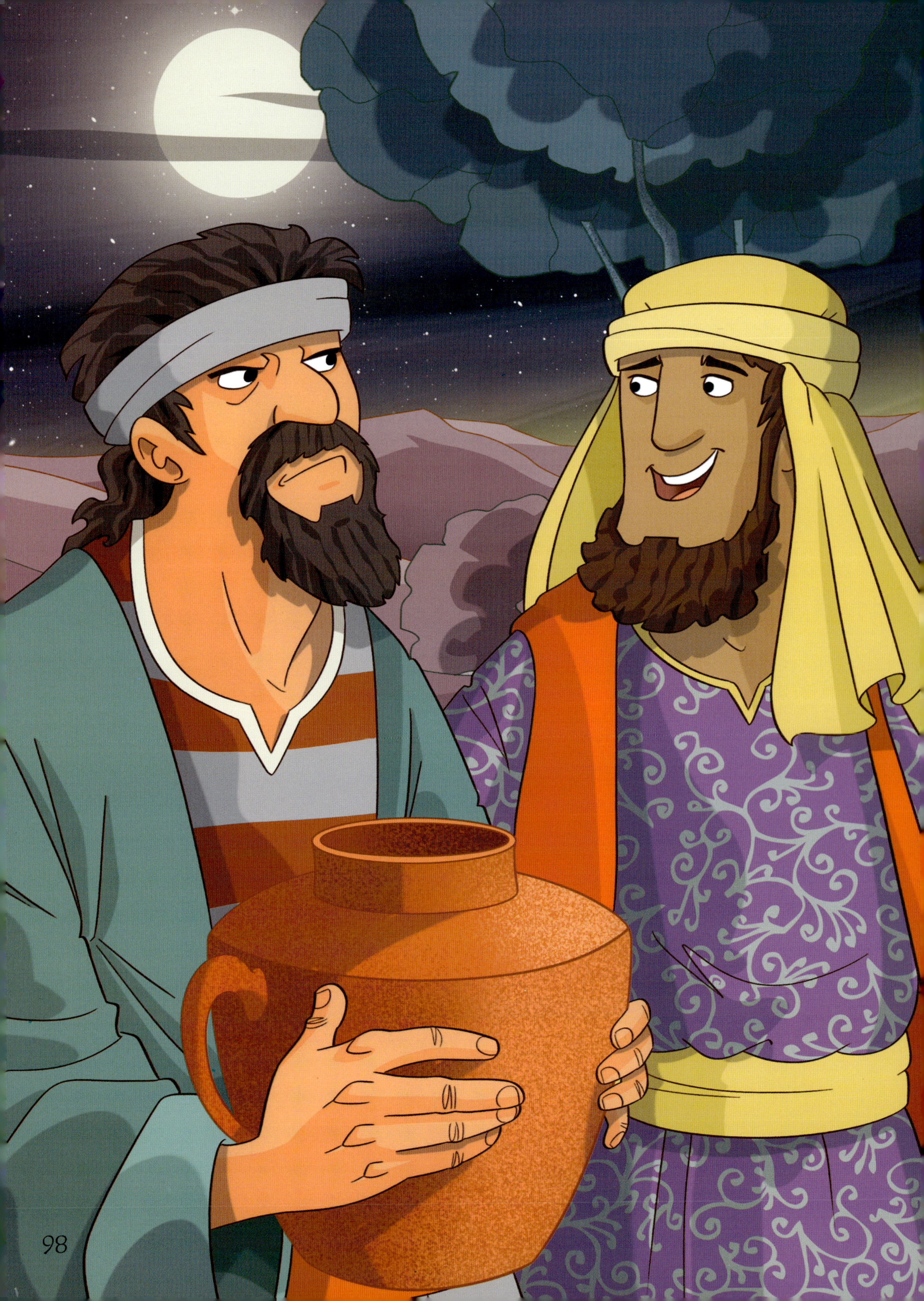

Now the older son, who had been working in the field, came home. "What's this all about?" he asked one of the servants. "Your brother has come home," replied the servant, "and your father has put on a great feast to celebrate."

This made the older brother really angry and he refused to join the party.

When the father asked why he was angry, the older son said, "All these years, I've been working hard and have never disobeyed you, yet you never gave me enough to have even a small feast with my friends! But now your son, who squandered your money on wild living, comes home, and you throw him a big party?"

The father replied, "Son, you are always with me, and everything I have is yours. But now it is time for celebration and happiness because your brother, whom we thought to be dead, has come home, alive! He was lost, but now he is found."

The Man Who Went Through the Roof

Mark 2:1–12

In the town of Caparnaum lived a man who couldn't walk. He was not able to work or care for himself. So, when Jesus came to Capernaum, his friends knew exactly what to do to help him.

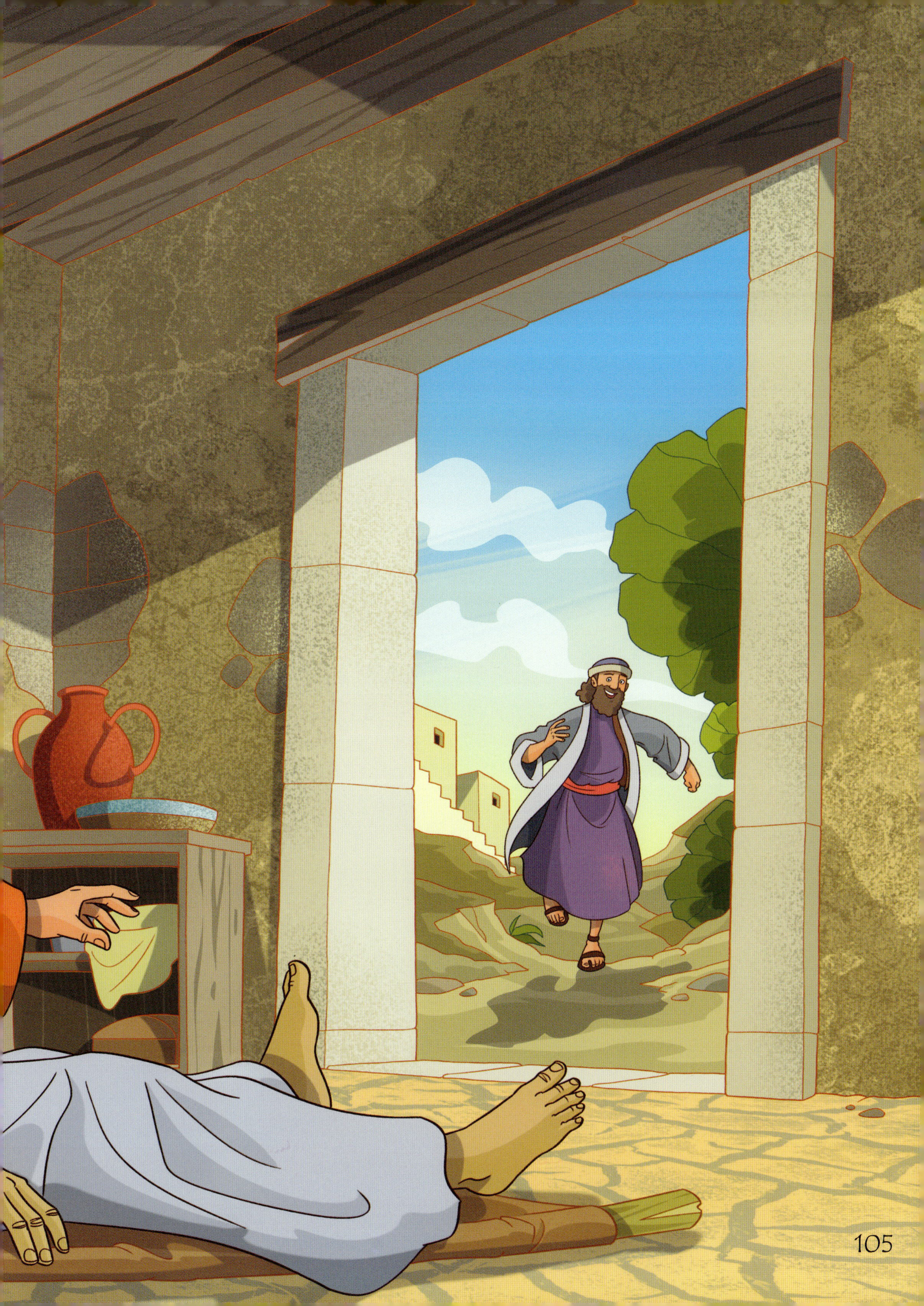

They carried him to Jesus on a mat. But, as they arrived to the house where Jesus was teaching, they couldn't get in because of the many people who had gathered to hear Jesus. So, they had an idea.

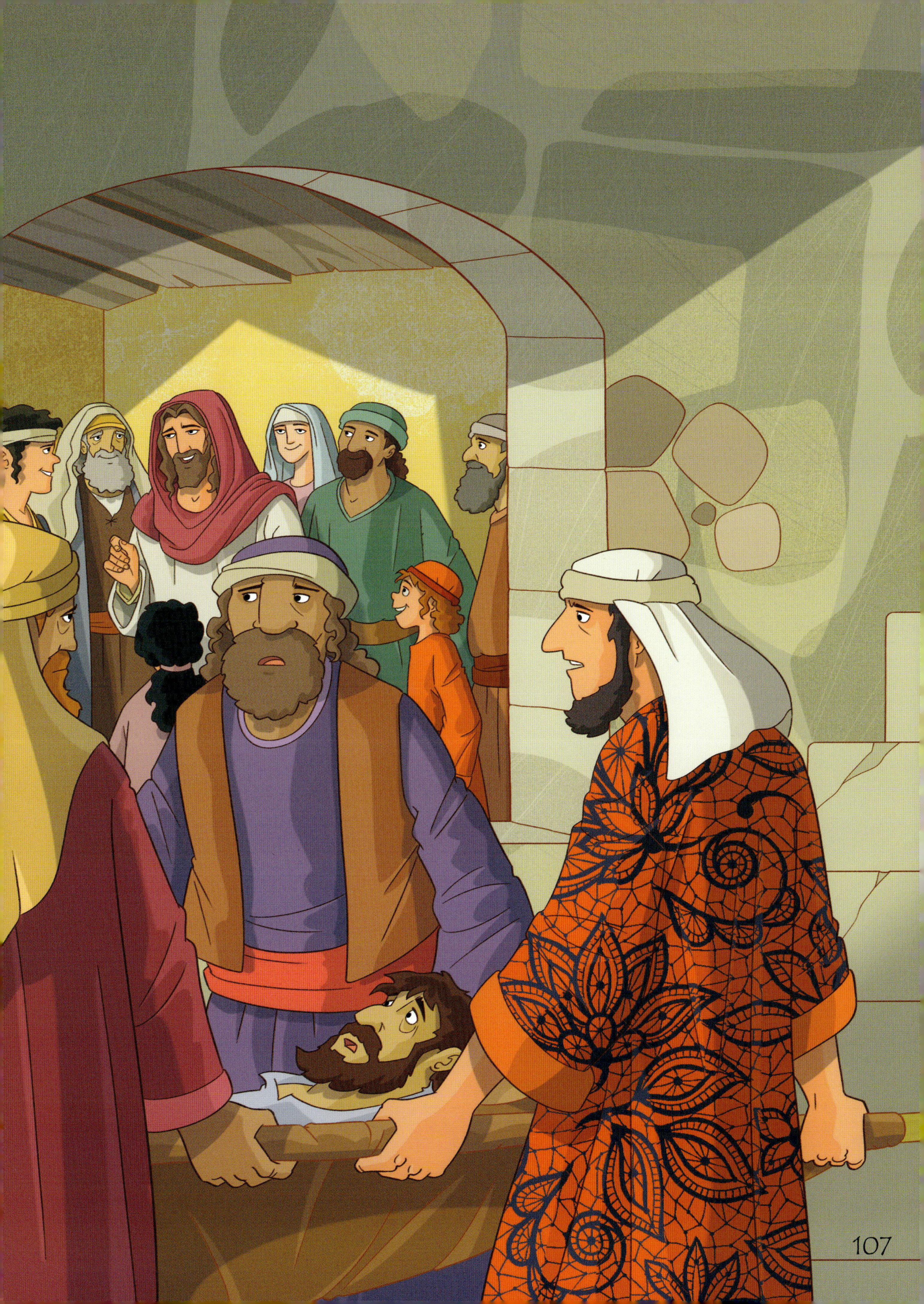

108

They took their friend up onto the roof, removed some of the roof tiles and lowered down their friend, right in front of Jesus. When Jesus saw their faith, He said, "Son, take heart, your sins are forgiven." Some religious teachers thought to themselves, "Why does this man talk this way? He is breaking our law! No one can forgive sins except God alone!"

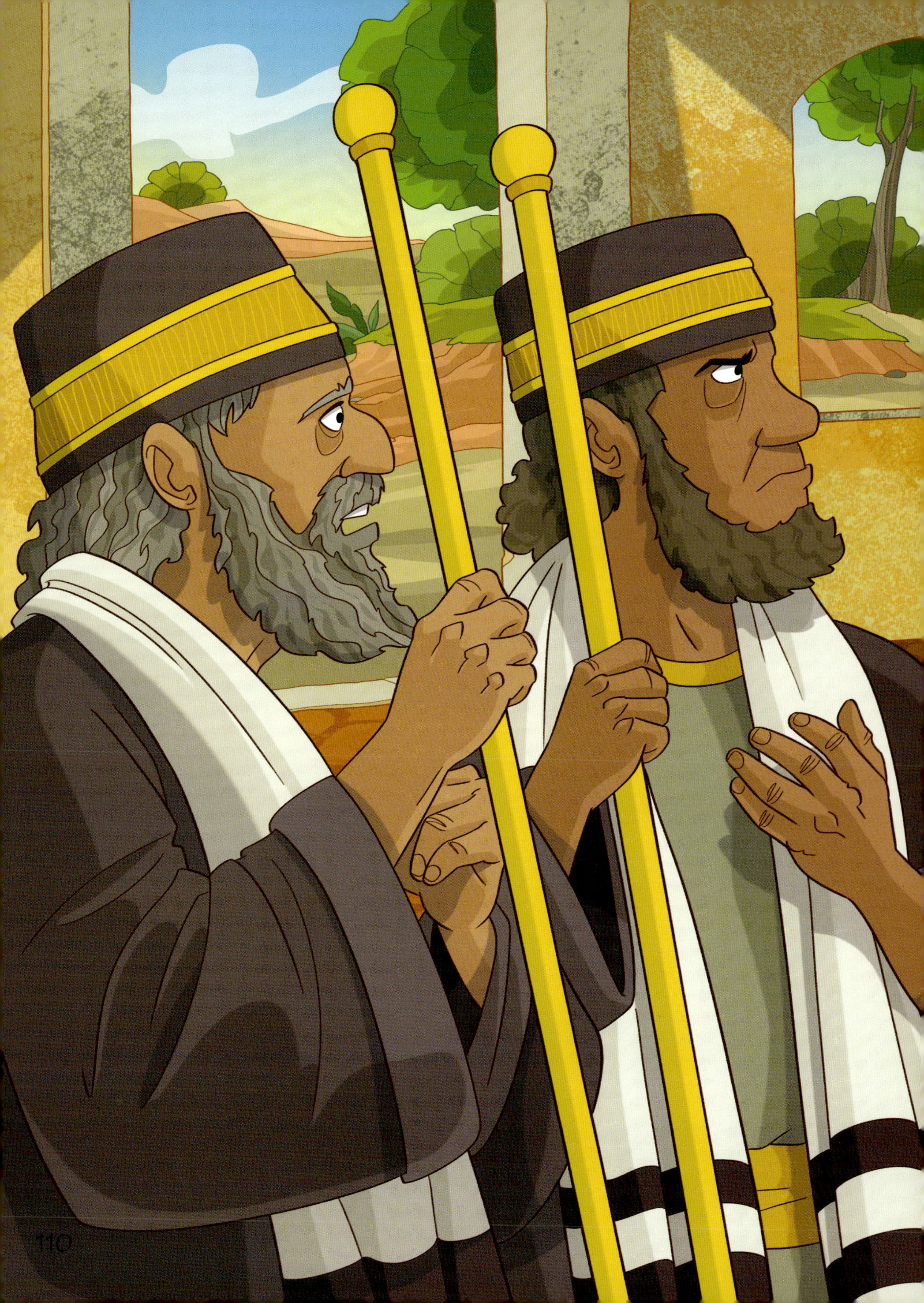

They were furious that Jesus was claiming to be God! But Jesus knew what these religious leaders were thinking, so He said to them, "Why are you thinking these things? Which is easier to say, 'Your sins are forgiven,' or simply, 'Get up, take your mat, and walk?'"

111

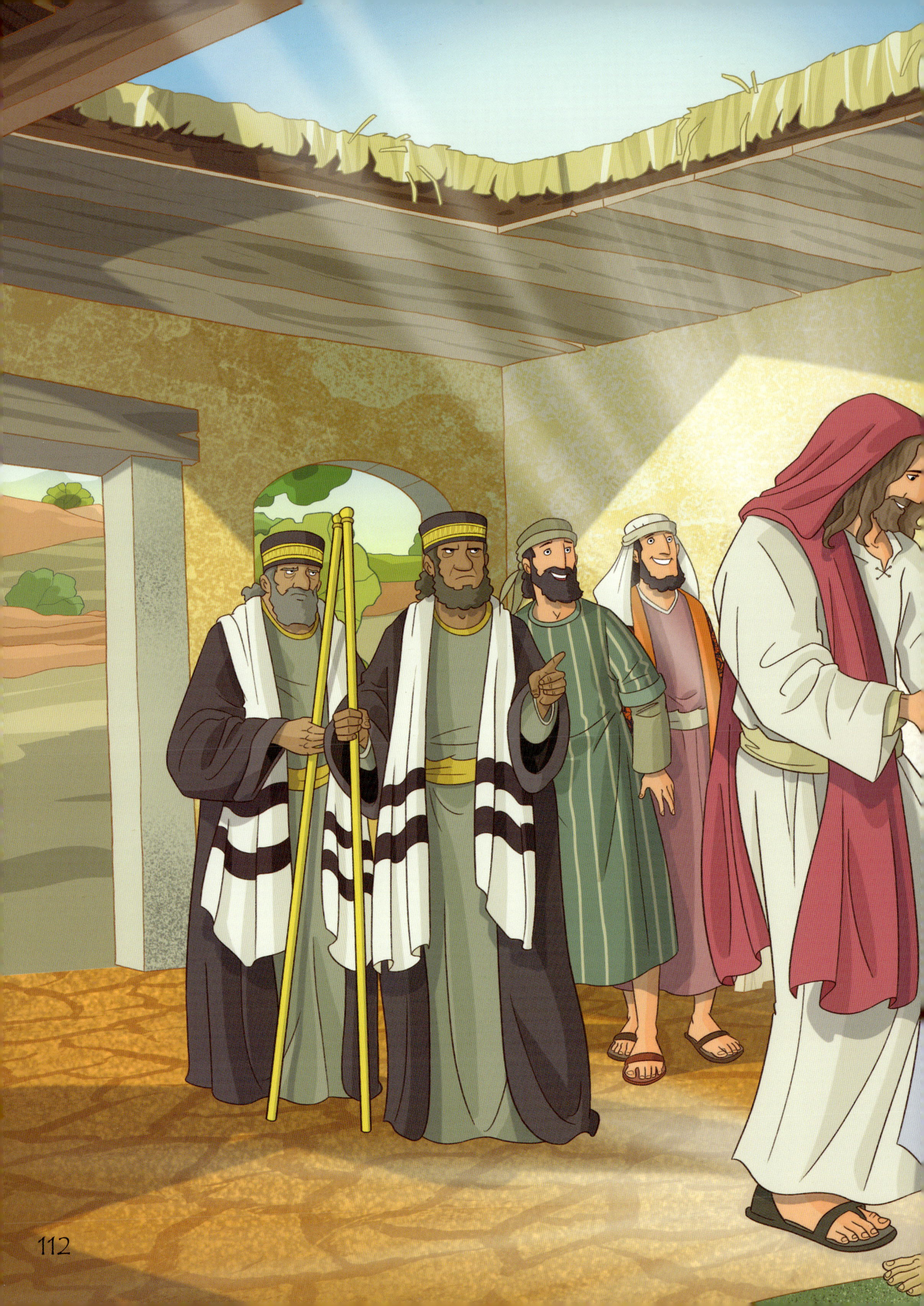

"For you to know that I have authority to forgive sins," Jesus said, "I say, get up, take your mat, and go home." The man immediately got up! This amazed everyone who saw it and they praised God. "We have never seen anything like this!" they said, as the man stood up, took his mat and walked out of the house, perfectly healed.

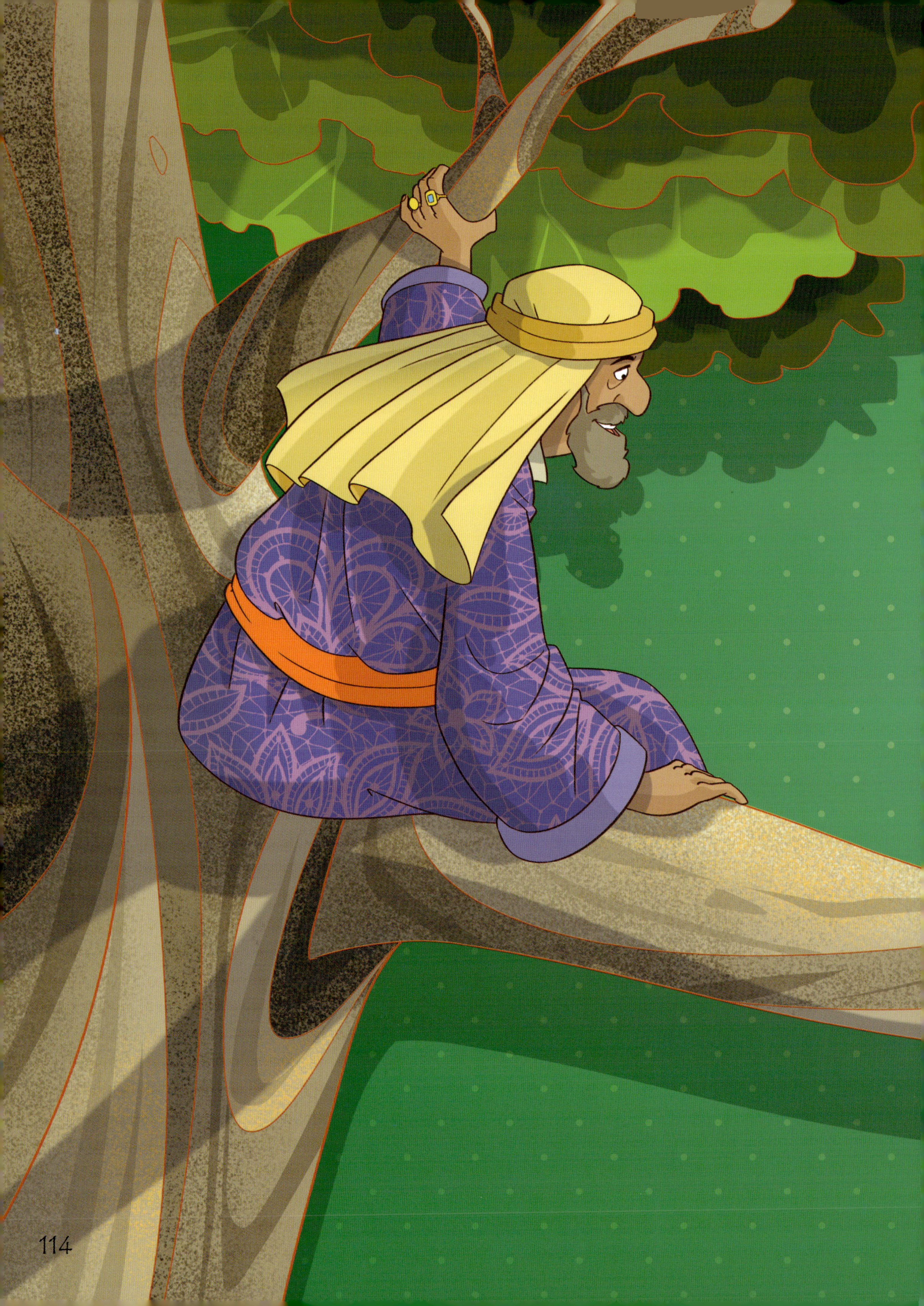

The Greedy Man Who Started to Share

Luke 19:1–10

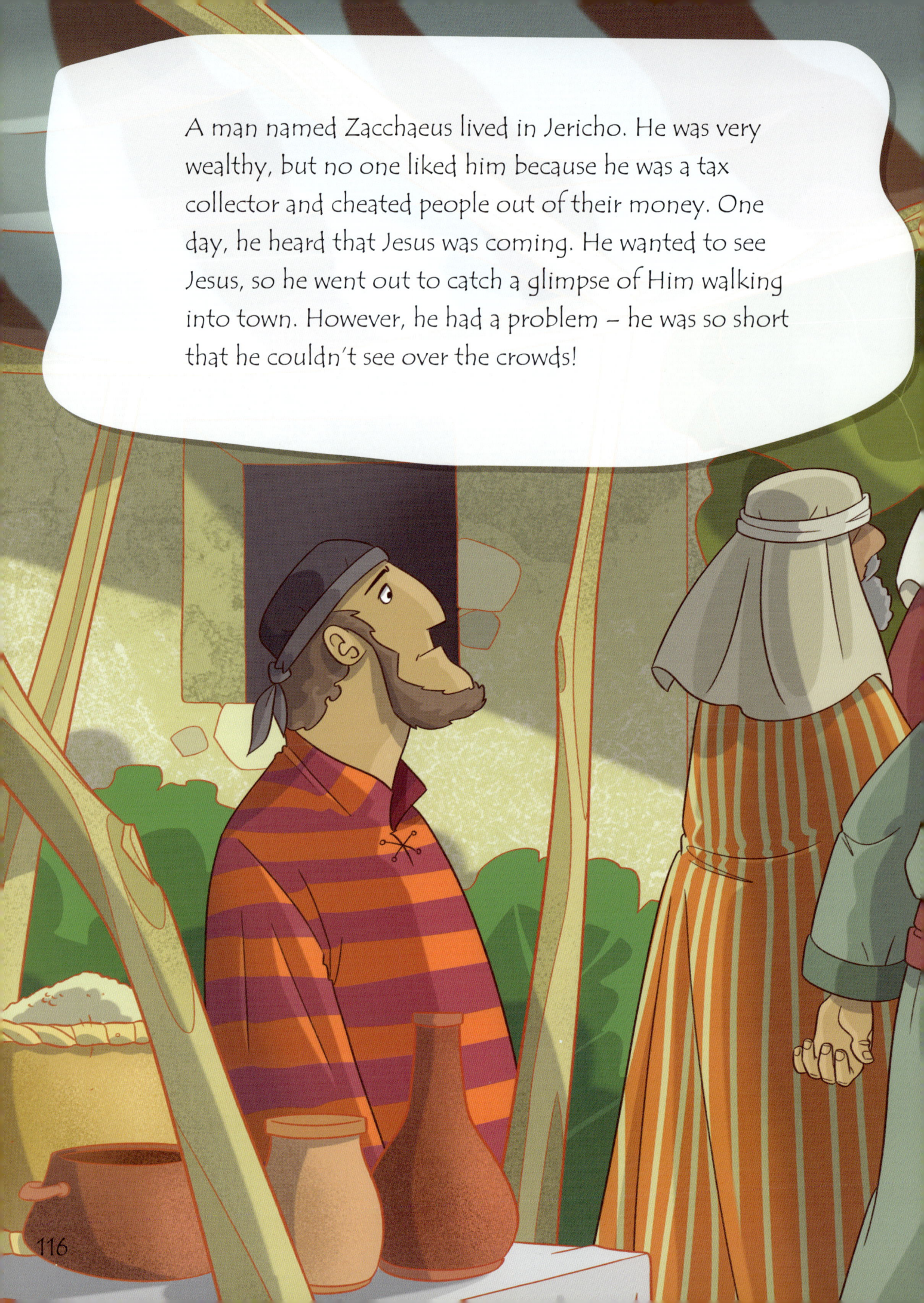

A man named Zacchaeus lived in Jericho. He was very wealthy, but no one liked him because he was a tax collector and cheated people out of their money. One day, he heard that Jesus was coming. He wanted to see Jesus, so he went out to catch a glimpse of Him walking into town. However, he had a problem – he was so short that he couldn't see over the crowds!

117

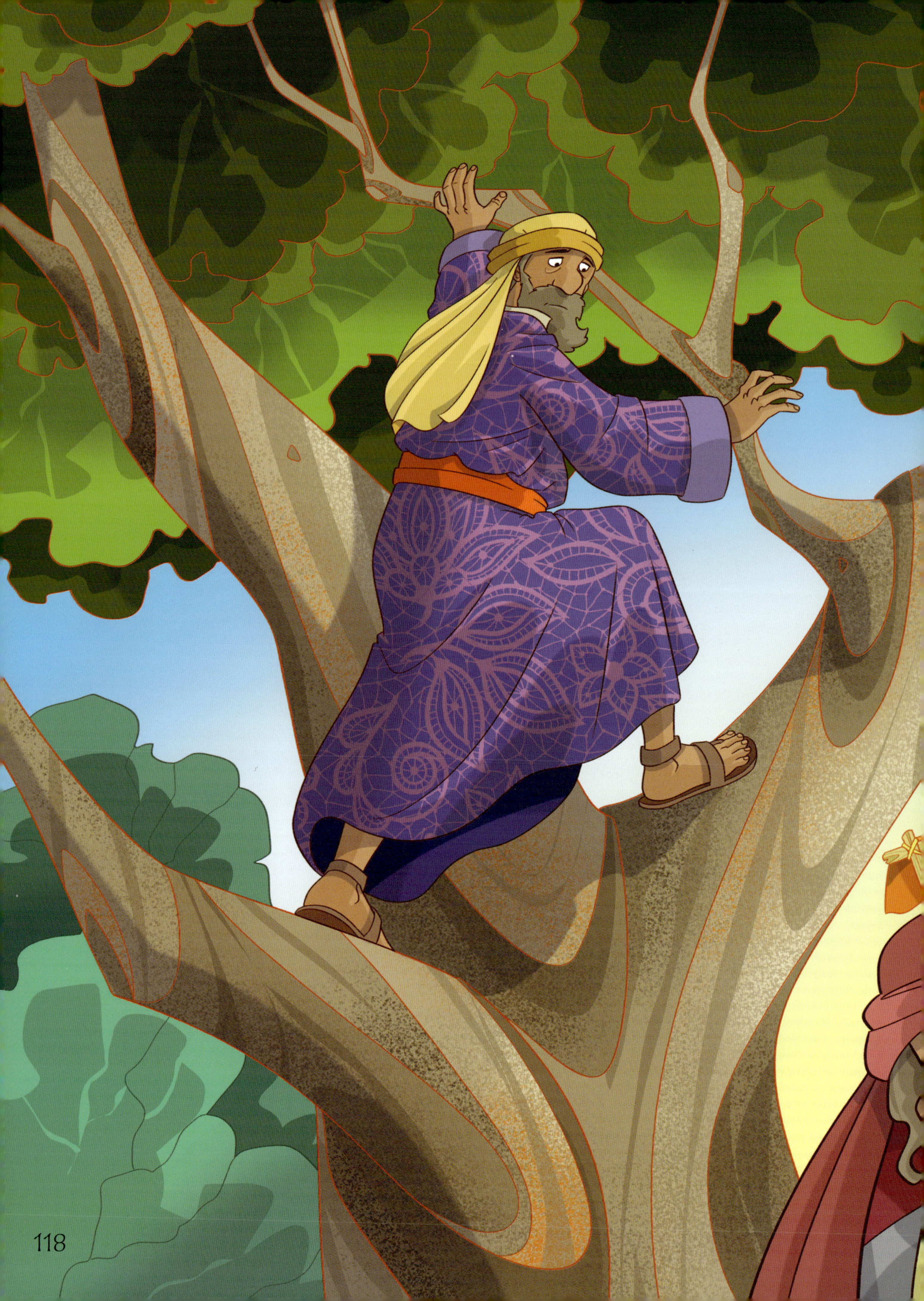

Then, Zacchaeus had an idea! He ran ahead of the crowd and found a sycamore tree. He climbed up into its branches so he could get a view of Jesus from there. Before long, he could see Jesus and His disciples as they were getting closer to where Zacchaeus sat perched in the tree.

When Jesus was right under the tree, He looked up and said to him, "Zacchaeus, come down from that tree. I would really love to come to your house today." Zacchaeus was amazed. Did Jesus really want to visit him? He hurried down so he could welcome Jesus to his home at once.

But when some of the other people saw this, they began to mutter, "He is going to the home of that sinner!"

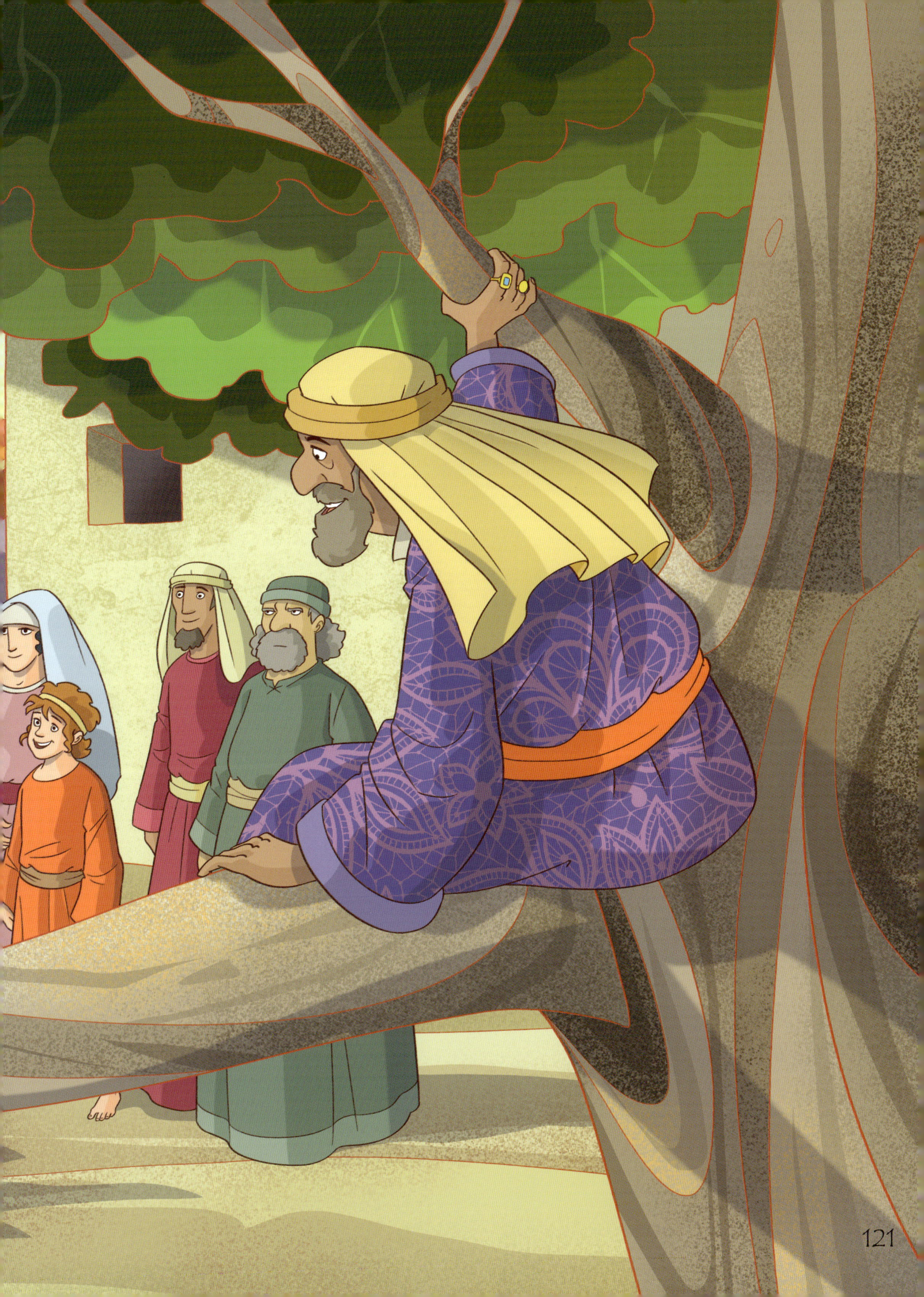

122

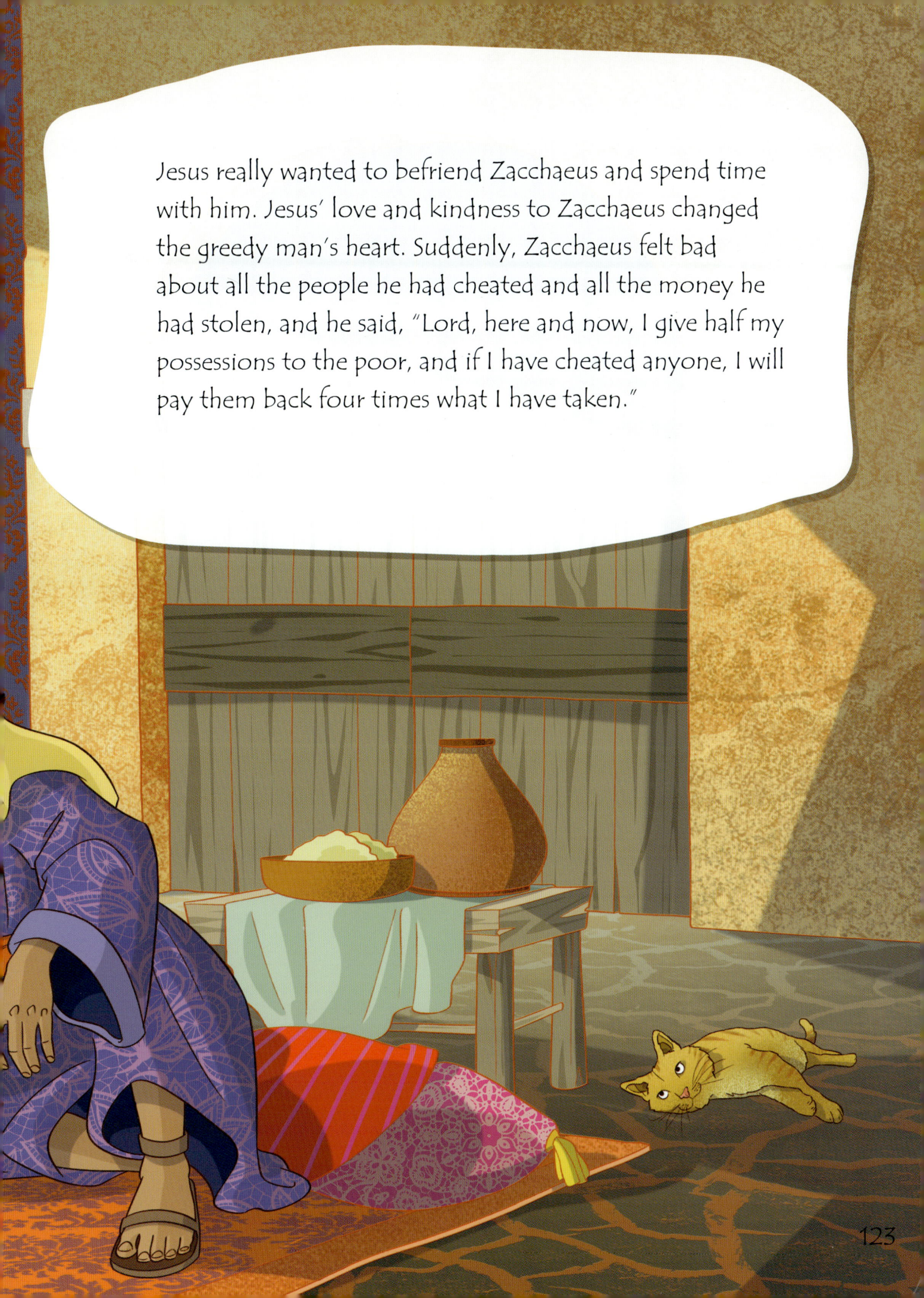

Jesus really wanted to befriend Zacchaeus and spend time with him. Jesus' love and kindness to Zacchaeus changed the greedy man's heart. Suddenly, Zacchaeus felt bad about all the people he had cheated and all the money he had stolen, and he said, "Lord, here and now, I give half my possessions to the poor, and if I have cheated anyone, I will pay them back four times what I have taken."

Jesus told everyone, "Today salvation has come to this man and his family, for it is people like him that I came to save." Jesus had forgiven Zacchaeus and he became a completely changed man. He repaid all the people whom he had stolen from or cheated. The greedy tax collector became the most generous and caring person in town!

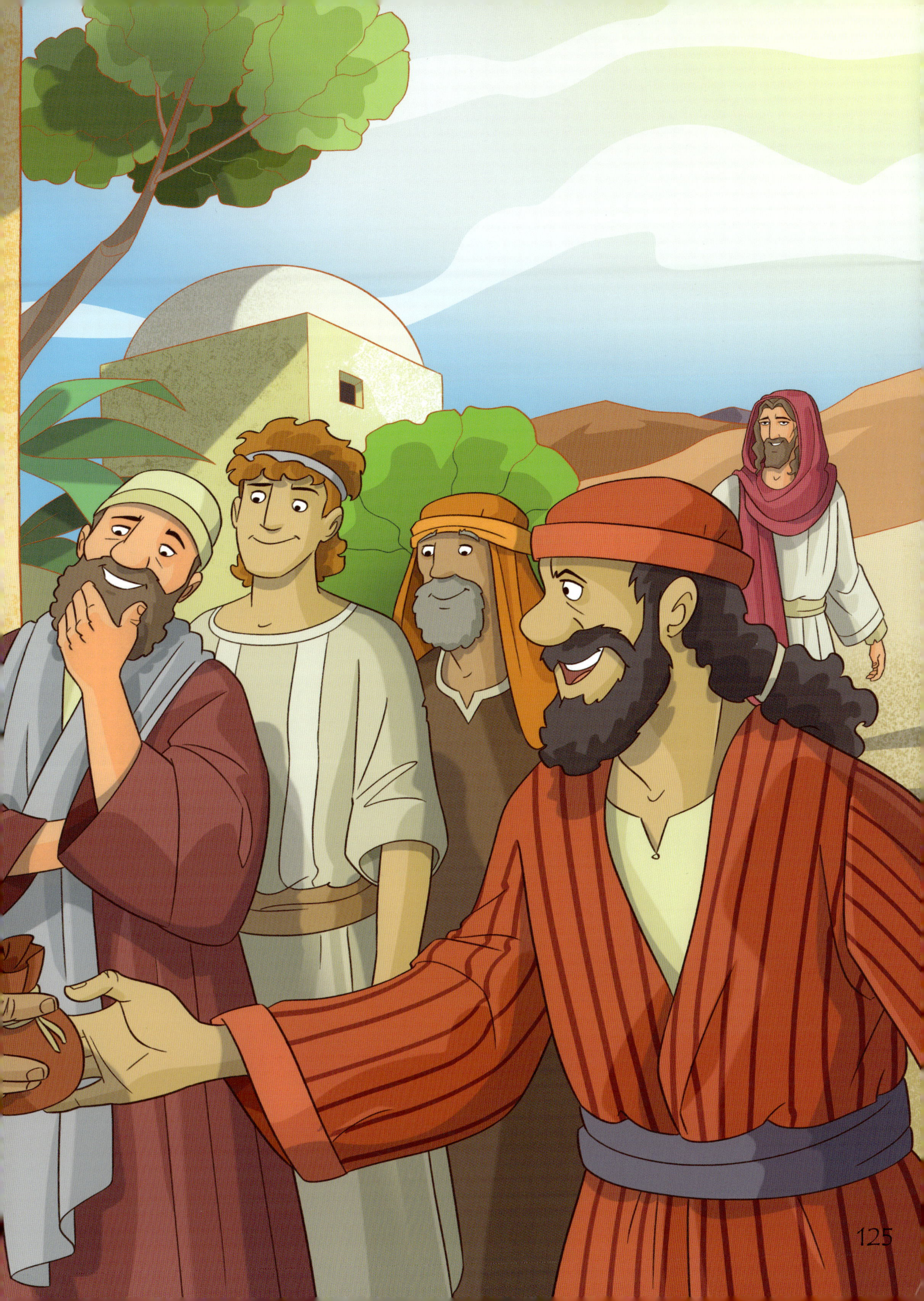

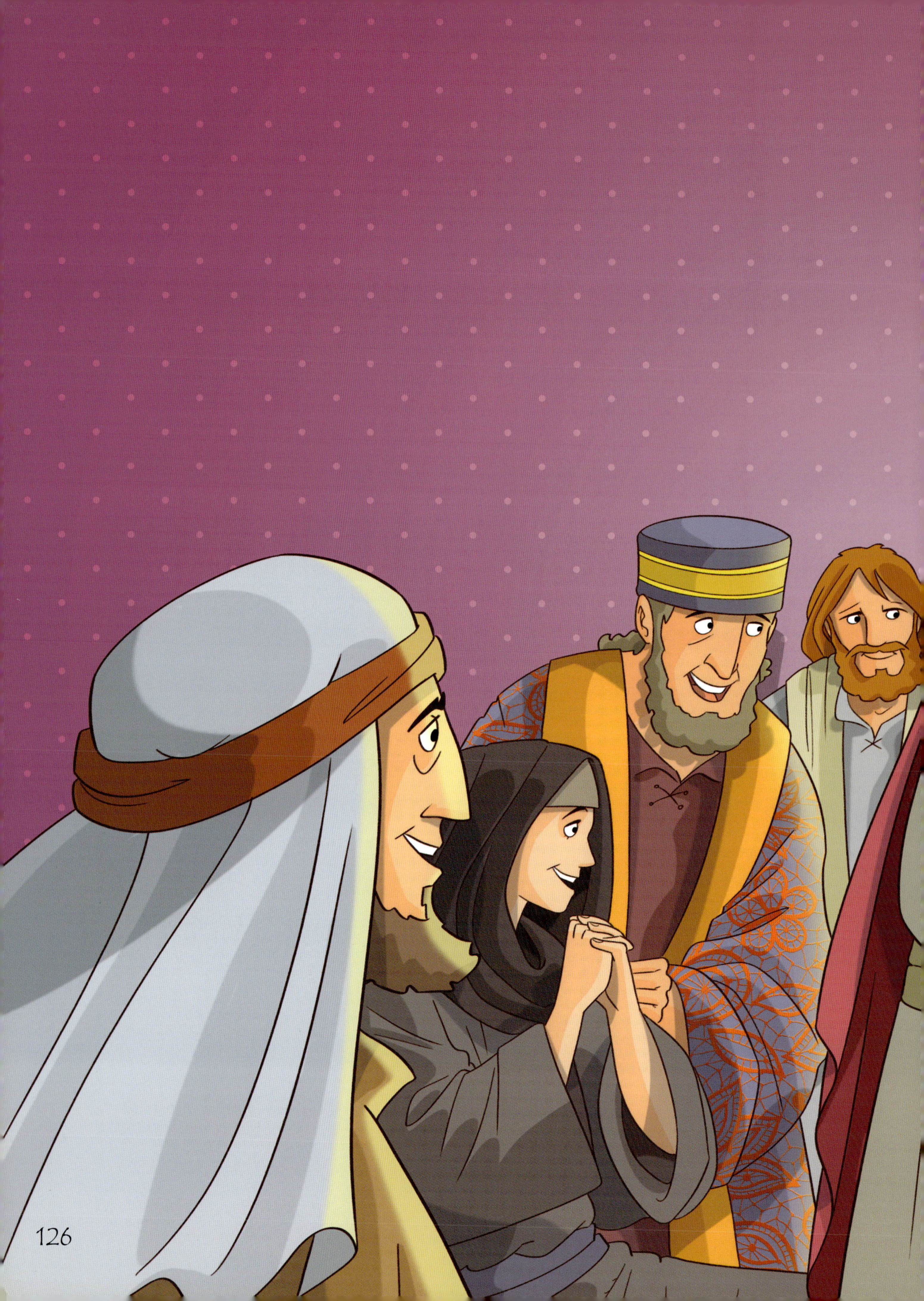

The Dead Girl Who Came Back to Life

Mark 5:21–43

127

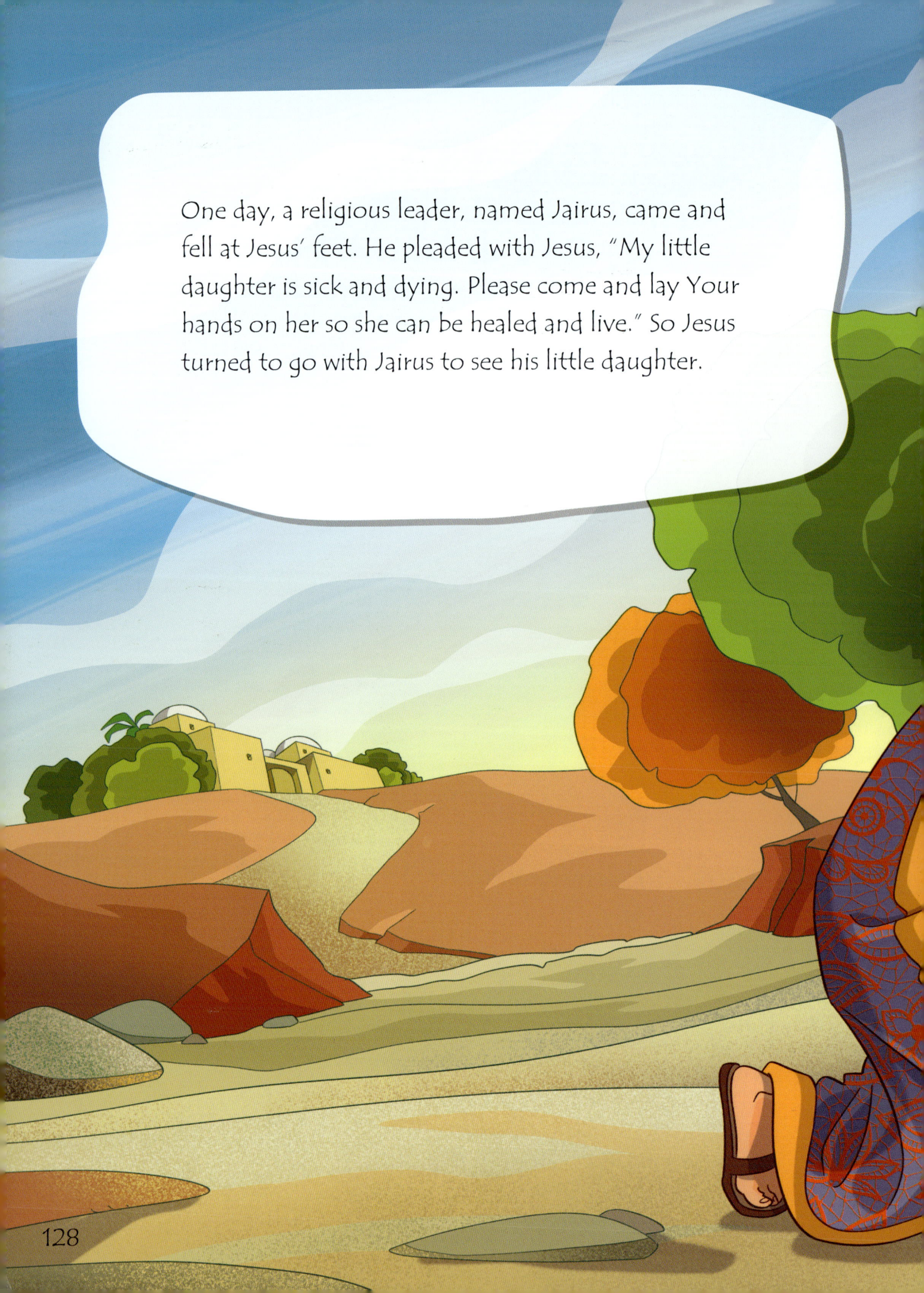

One day, a religious leader, named Jairus, came and fell at Jesus' feet. He pleaded with Jesus, "My little daughter is sick and dying. Please come and lay Your hands on her so she can be healed and live." So Jesus turned to go with Jairus to see his little daughter.

129

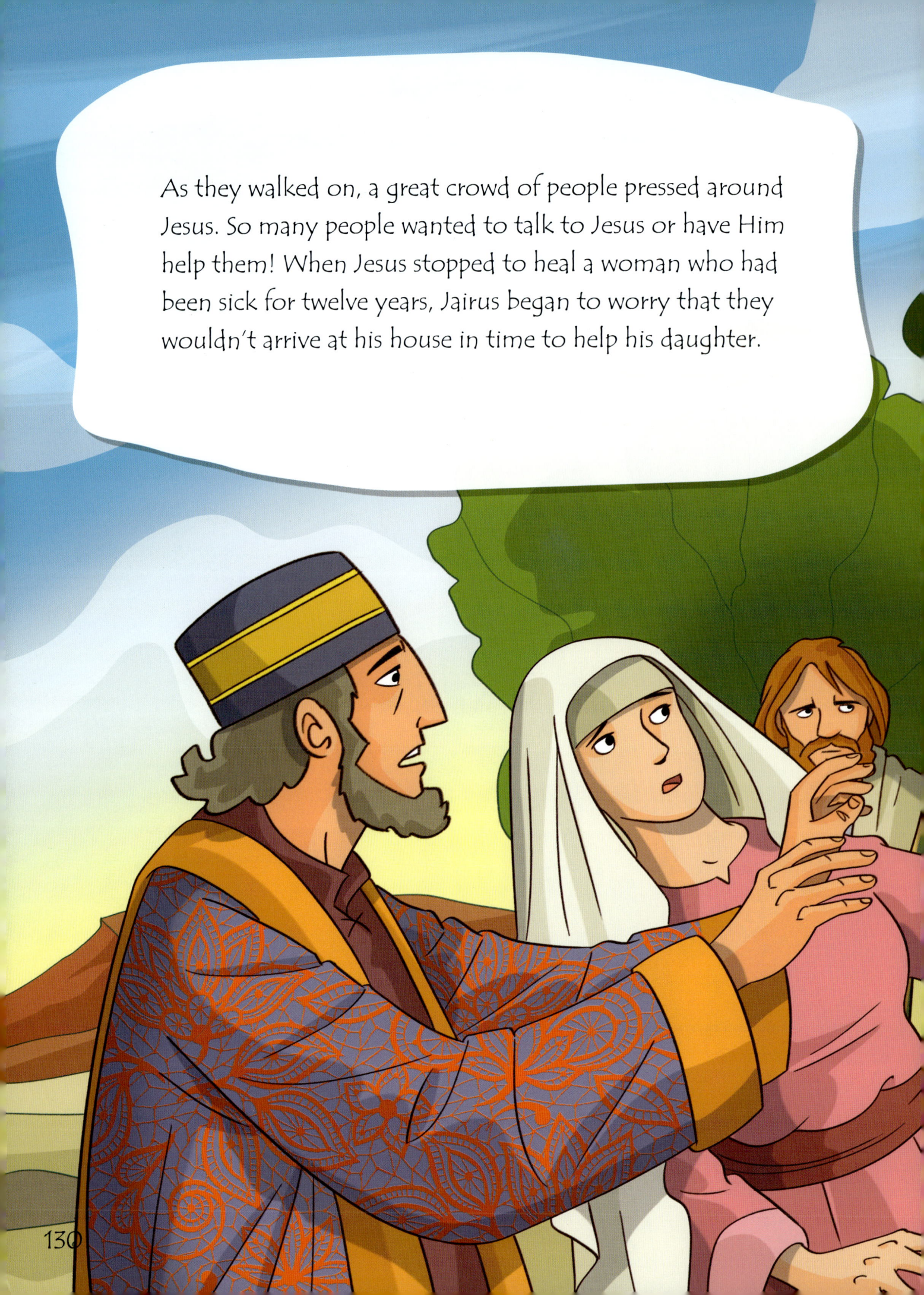

As they walked on, a great crowd of people pressed around Jesus. So many people wanted to talk to Jesus or have Him help them! When Jesus stopped to heal a woman who had been sick for twelve years, Jairus began to worry that they wouldn't arrive at his house in time to help his daughter.

131

At that moment, some people came from Jairus's house. "Your daughter is dead," they said. "Tell Jesus not to come. It's too late."

Jesus overheard them and said to Jairus, "Don't be afraid. Just believe and have faith." Jesus left the crowd and followed Jairus to his home.

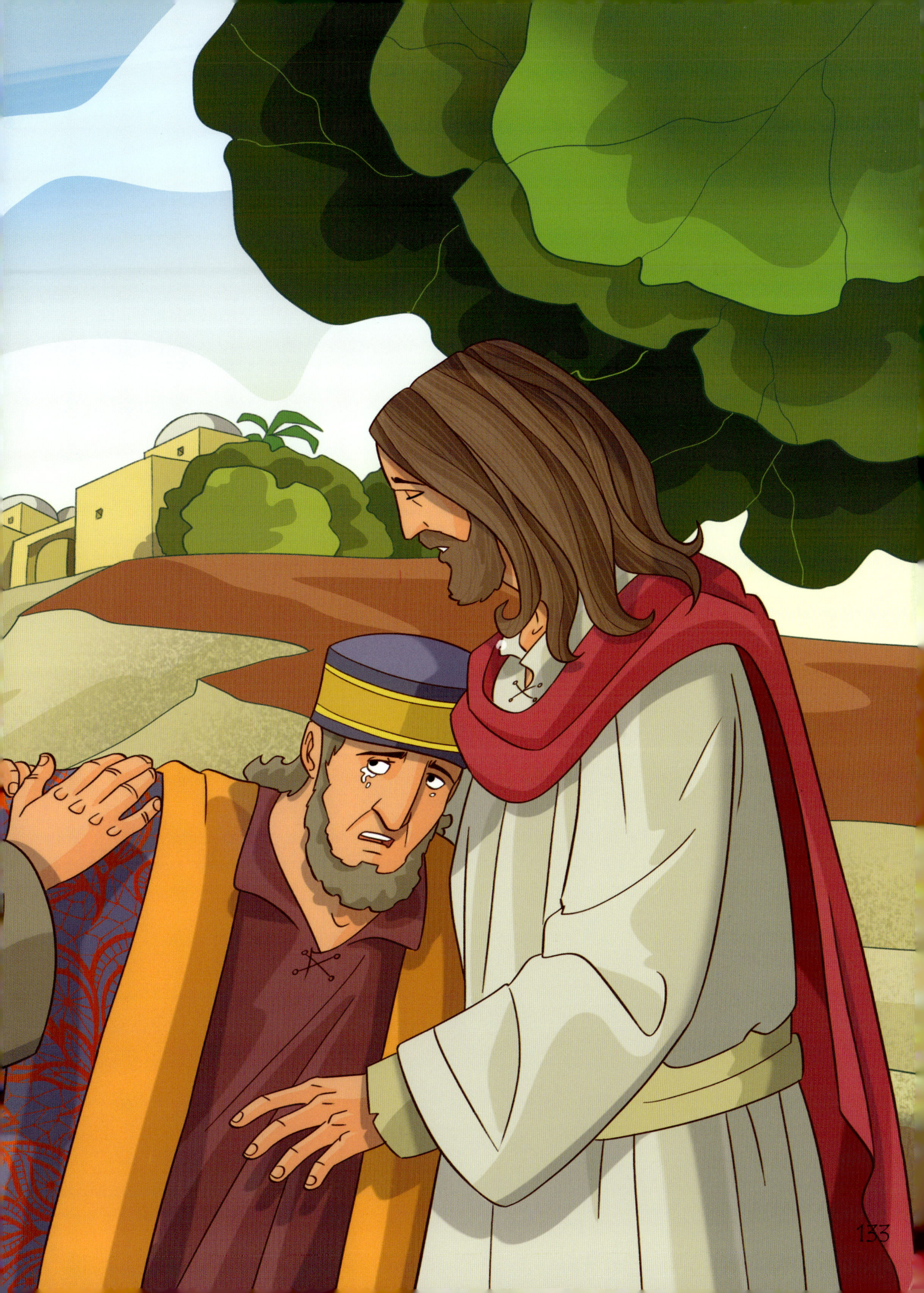

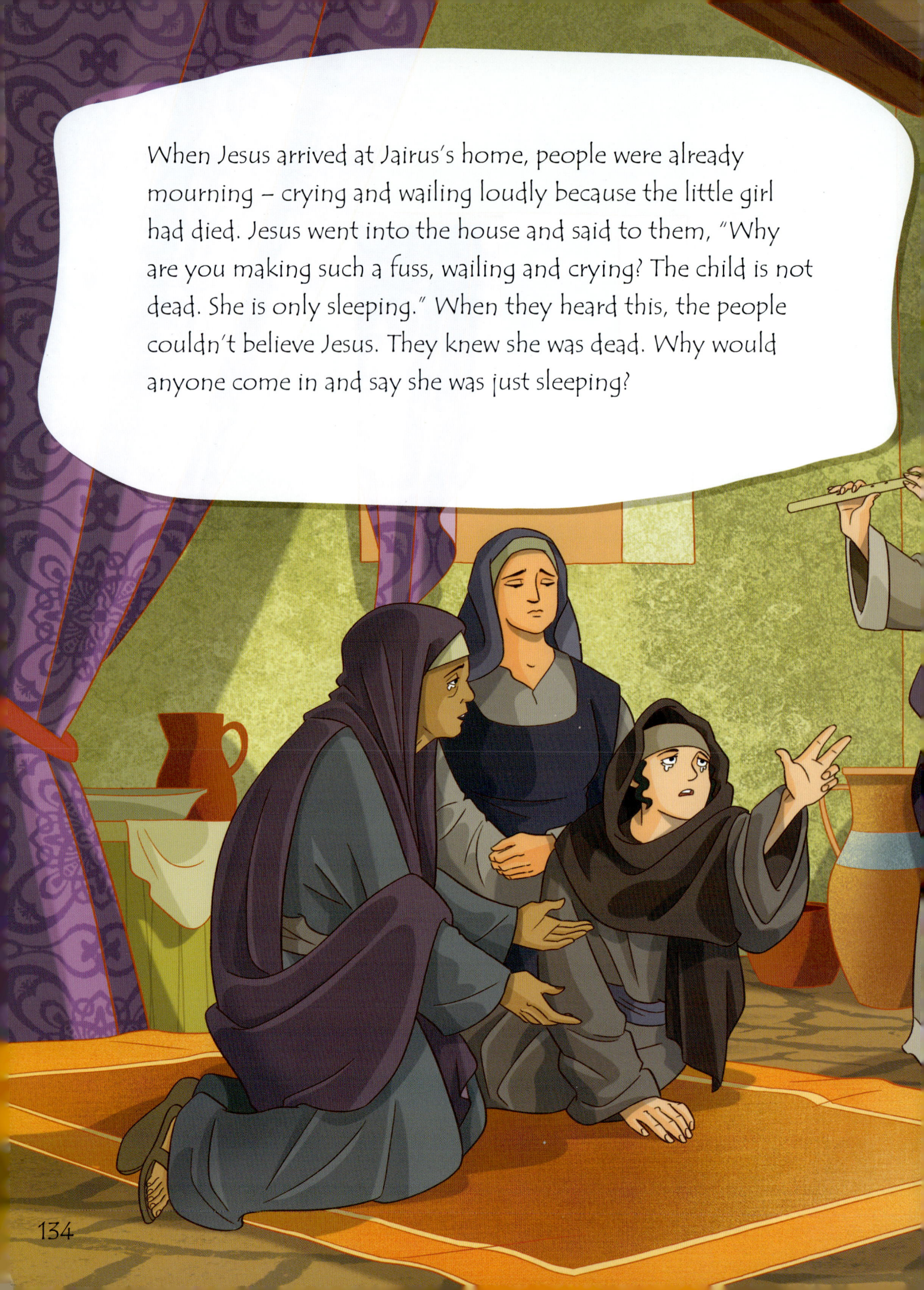

When Jesus arrived at Jairus's home, people were already mourning – crying and wailing loudly because the little girl had died. Jesus went into the house and said to them, "Why are you making such a fuss, wailing and crying? The child is not dead. She is only sleeping." When they heard this, the people couldn't believe Jesus. They knew she was dead. Why would anyone come in and say she was just sleeping?

135

Jesus sent the people out of the house, and He took the child's father and mother, along with Peter, James, and John, into the little girl's room. He gently took her hand and said to her, "Little girl, get up!"

137

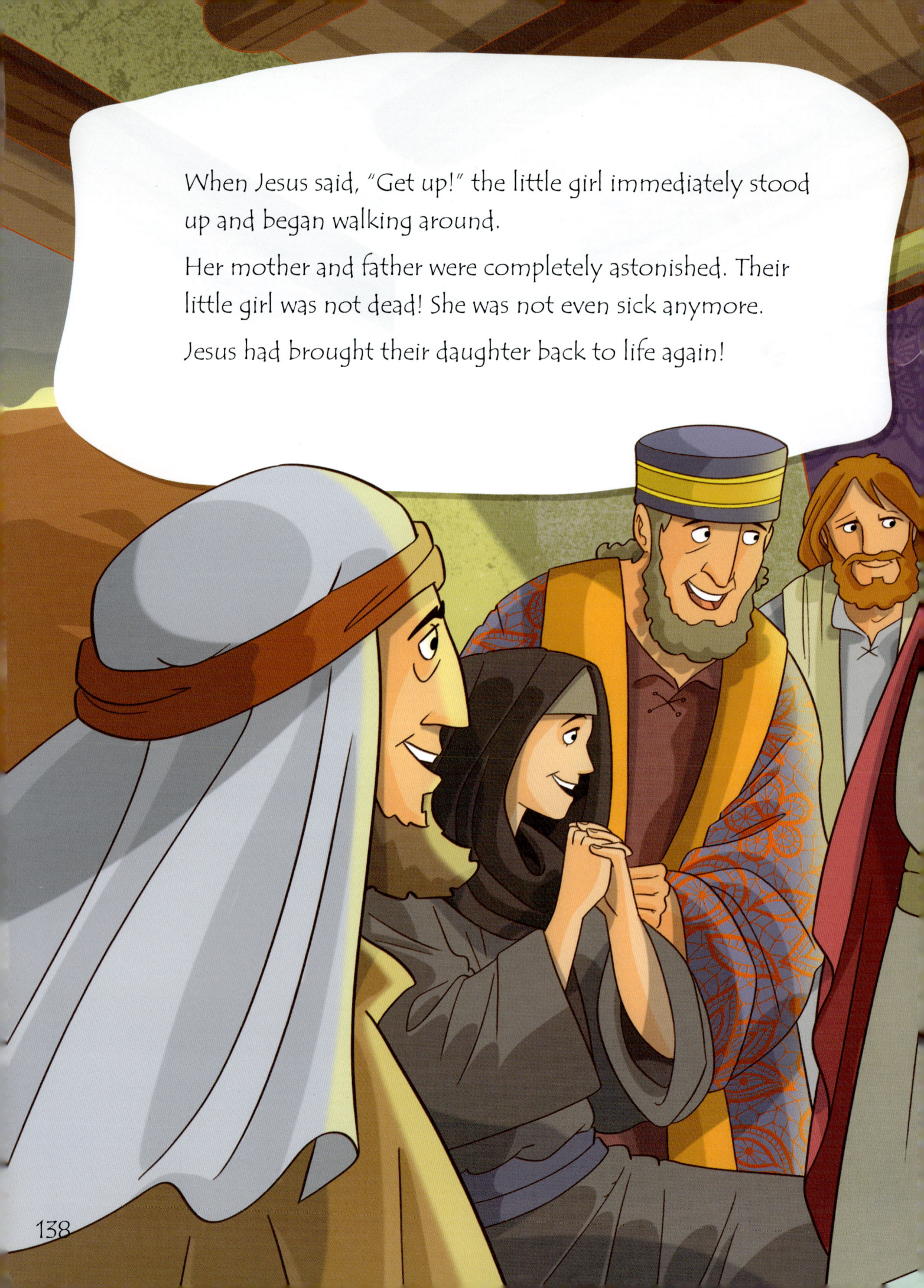

When Jesus said, "Get up!" the little girl immediately stood up and began walking around.

Her mother and father were completely astonished. Their little girl was not dead! She was not even sick anymore.

Jesus had brought their daughter back to life again!

139